Defending Catholicism

# Defending Catholicism

A Concise Defense of Catholicism from the Bible
against Classic Protestant Objections

James S. Anderson

WIPF & STOCK · Eugene, Oregon

DEFENDING CATHOLICISM
A Concise Defense of Catholicism from the Bible Against Classic
Protestant Objections

Wipf & Stock
An Imprint of Wipf and Stock Publishers
199 W. 8th Ave., Suite 3
Eugene, OR 97401

www.wipfandstock.com

PAPERBACK ISBN: 978-1-5326-8903-1
HARDCOVER ISBN: 978-1-5326-8904-8
EBOOK ISBN: 978-1-5326-8905-5

Manufactured in the U.S.A.

In loving memory of Guadalupe "Mita" Peña
and William C. Peña

# Contents

*Introduction* | ix

I. Scripture, Tradition & Apostolic Succession | 1

II. The Papacy | 10

III. Purgatory | 17

IV. The Real Presence of Christ in the Eucharist | 22

V. The Virgin Mary & the Saints | 36

VI. The Sacraments, Specifically the Sacrament
of Reconciliation | 49

VII. Not by Faith Alone | 59

Conclusion | 73

*Bibliography* | 79

# Introduction

COUNTLESS, HELPFUL AND ERUDITE Catholic apologetic book treatments have been done addressing Protestant objections to Catholicism and are commended to the reader; however, a short monograph on the subject by way of a summary of the salient refutations of Protestant objections to the faith is in order.[1] As time constraints preclude many in our busy world today of the time to delve into the helpful books on the important subject, a concise summary refuting the main Protestant objections to Catholicism is necessary and perhaps even lacking. The Bible, as well as the early church, not only demonstrate the main Protestant Reformation tenets incorrect but prove and support the doctrines of Catholicism, the only church today, along with the Orthodox, that can claim to go back all the way to Christ himself, according to the Catholic doctrine of apostolic succession. No Protestant denomination can claim this. What follows is not an exhaustive treatment of the subject. Rather, it serves as a helpful primer for anyone wanting to know how to answer Protestant brothers and sisters with quick, simple responses from Scripture, in virtually every instance, for most of their hang-ups, all the while revealing Catholicism to be the original church possessing the fullness of the faith, the one true holy and apostolic church.

---

1. Protestant literally means "one who protests."

# Chapter I

# Scripture, Tradition &
# Apostolic Succession

THE REFORMATION RALLYING CRY *sola Scriptura*, simply put, is not a biblical doctrine. Nowhere does such a teaching appear in the Bible![1] Scripture plus tradition,[2] the Catholic position, actually is, according to the Bible. Second Thessalonians 2:15 reads, "So then, brothers and sisters, stand firm and hold fast to the traditions that you were taught by us, either by word of mouth or by our letter."[3] "By mouth" affirms traditions passed on orally, not emanating

---

1. This point in no way contradictions 2 Timothy 3:16: "All scripture is inspired by God and is useful for teaching, for reproof, for correction, and for training in righteousness." One need remember when this text was written Scripture did not mean the canon of texts we now call the Bible. Catholics believe Scripture in fact to be inspired and useful for teaching; however, it needs to be noted this text does not preclude the vital importance of tradition in any manner. Tradition gave us Scripture and the Bible explicitly explains the importance of tradition, as will be explicated presently. One issue under the surface between different Christian groups is the meaning of "inspired," as there is not a consensus on what this means between differing religious traditions. How it is defined has huge implications and different Christian traditions obviously understand it quite differently. It is fair to say Catholics view it as its actual definition suggests as opposed to viewing it as suggesting every text and word of Scripture is infallible and inerrant, a rather naïve, tenuous positon anyone with some training in the Bible realizes is not sustainable.

2. Tradition here in regards to Catholicism is analogous in many ways to "Oral Torah" or "Oral Law" in Rabbinic Judaism.

3. All Scripture references in this work are taken from the NRSV translation of the Bible.

always from a written document, much less a sacred collection of texts. The canon[4] of Scripture would take hundreds of years before it was agreed upon, centuries after this text in 2 Thessalonians was written. Thus, the early church passed the traditions on orally as well as via documents, though early churches usually had only a few of the documents that would later be contained in the New Testament, and well as some that would not make it into the canon of Scripture. It must be understood that the early church for centuries did not have a Bible; rather, each different small church community in a differing region, mostly comprised within the Roman Empire, likely only had a gospel and maybe a letter or two of Paul. The Catholic Church much later gives us a canon (measuring rod, norm, collection of rules) of Scripture or the Bible. Since the early Church did not have the canon of Scripture we have today for hundreds of years, tradition was thus important, as it still is today. The early churches thus did not have Scripture but one or two texts for hundreds of years in different communities. Therefore, it was about the tradition passed on not a written text. Our written texts are tradition.

Additionally, simply put—those who accept Scripture accept the tradition of the Catholic Church, as the church gave us Scripture. How ironic for many Protestants. It is tradition that gave us Scripture and decided what constitutes Scripture. By accepting the Bible a Protestant implicitly accepts the Catholic Church, as the Catholic Church gave us the Bible.[5] Most likely have not even

4. Canon simply means a measuring stick by which something is measured.

5. On the canonization of the Bible, one should see the helpful collection of essays edited by Lee M. McDonald and James S. Sanders, *The Canon Debate* (Peabody: Hendrickson, 2002) and Paul D. Wegner, *The Journey from Texts to Translations: The Origin and Development of the Bible* (Grand Rapids: Baker, 1999). The canonization of Scripture was not the church saying here is what is authoritative—believe it, but rather the Church saying this is what has been authoritative for churches throughout the years and the texts we believe go back to early times and to the disciples in some close manner, ether to a disciple or one who was with a disciple of Christ. It is noteworthy and important that all texts in the New Testament were likely written anywhere from 45 years to150 years after Jesus walked the earth. From a historian's point of view, that is impressive and important, the theory being the closer in time to an event a text

taken the time to realize this fact and that the notion of Scripture alone and not church tradition, so common among the vast majority of Protestants today, is not tenable or historical, for tradition and the Catholic church gave us the Bible.

The Catholic Apologist Trent Horn writes, "The canon of Scripture was first declared in Rome in AD 382 and was later defined at two Catholic councils in North Africa (Hippo in AD 393 and Carthage in AD 397)," and later at the Council of Trent (1545–1563) as part of the Counterreformation in reaction to the Protestant Reformation.[6] Protestants today are actually still missing several books of Scripture, thus several teachings, such as a rather explicit reference in 2 Maccabees to purgatory addressed below. Interestingly and brazenly, Martin Luther, the founder of the Protestant movement in the sixteenth century actually wanted the book of James thrown out of the Bible[7] because it did not fit with his subjective, private interpretations of sacred Scripture and theology. That private interpretations of texts are a problem will be addressed below and that God's providence did not allow for James to be expunged from the Bible must be thought of as a blessing, for it is a treasure of information in a rather short letter. Karl Barth, a twentieth-century Protestant theologian of the Reformed tradition, who Pope Pius XII said was the "greatest theologian since Thomas Aquinas," said the Bible does its job if it points to Christ. As Christians, we do not want to make the Bible into an idol, which is much less of a danger in the Catholic Church, especially when tradition exists to help temper this possibility, a tradition that passes on how the canon actually came together.

---

purports to discuss the more likely it is originally. This is a sound theory. The Hebrew Bible is a different case, as its texts are much older and written much later than the events they purport to describe. Also, history writing does not exist until the time of Herodotus in the Hellenist era; thus is it fair to anachronistically apply our modern standards back onto ancients who did not have the same standards for history writing? The New Testament is a different matter altogether because history writing did exist buy the time its texts were written.

6. Horn, *Why We're Catholic*, 78. Also see endnote 68 on page 228 regarding the ecumenical Council of Trent.

7. He referred to James as the "book of straw."

The history of the canonization of the Bible and really the Church for that matter is not all that well-known to most Protestants. The convert and Cardinal John Henry Newman said, "To be deep in history is to cease to be a Protestant."[8] Protestants tend to skip roughly 1400 years of history, though they do like St. Augustine. In a Presbyterian seminary, the present author received a robust theological education to include both biblical languages and much more, but only one class in Church history. However, the old yet impressive, classic textbook in which the first addition was originally published one hundred years ago entitled: *A History of the Christian Church*[9] was used. Thus, Protestants are often want, especially the laity, in their knowledge of tradition and the teaching of the early church, even immediately following the disciples, which confirms all the topics and doctrines addressed here, such as the real presence of Christ in the Eucharist or the place of Mary in the Church.

A salient aspect in Catholicism that can only be claimed by the Catholic faith, as well as the Orthodox (some might argue Episcopalians too, but most Catholics would not be at ease with the validity of this claim) is the supremely important teaching/doctrine of apostolic succession. It follows from Christ instituting the church (Matt 16:13–19) and subsequently giving power to his successors/disciples to carry on his work imbibed with keys of the church, power to bind in heaven (Matt 16:13–20), ability to forgive and retain sins (John 20:22–23) and so on. It is only logical that upon the death of the disciples, their roles would be passed on to the leaders of the Church up into today and until the Second Coming. How else would the church survive, a church Christ clearly established and desired, as opposed to those today who think and argue Christ did not want, desire or establish an instituted Church? Scripture contradicts this. The authority passed on to the leaders

8. I was reminded of this popular quote by Patrick Madrid, *Why Be Catholic: Ten Answers to a Very Important Question* (New York: Image, 2014), 34. In the endnotes #7 on p. 211 he cites Newman's "An Essay on the Development of Christian Doctrine," 7.

9. Williston Walker, Richard A. Norris, David W. Lotz and Robert T. Handy, *A History of the Christian Church* (4th ed., New York: Scribner, 1985).

does so through the office of the bishops of the Church. Bishops then give authority to priests, but apostolic succession authority is through the bishops. That a bishop can and often is fallible in no way negates the validity of his official work and duties, authority or validity of the sacraments he oversees, such as overseeing ordinations, confirmation, marriages or presiding over the Eucharist. This important point was addressed early on in the Donatism heresy.[10] It often takes heresy to address issues in the church, as it often takes issues to address and implement secular laws.

Apostolic succession ensures the Church continues the work of God and grants the Church via the bishops a means of safeguarding the tradition and depository of the faith, such as from heresies (e.g., Marcionism, Donatism, and Gnosticism). Around 95 CE the then Bishop of Rome wrote in 1 Clement that the bishops were the successors of the disciples/apostles, displaying this belief very early, even before all the New Testament had been written. Saint Irenaeus, the second-century bishop of Lyon too affirmed this belief. Thus, Christ established a church, as will be seen below when addressing the papacy and the famous text in which he declares Peter the first pope. His church serves as the possessor of the depository of faith given by Christ and this truth and his teachings are passed on through the bishops in an unbroken chain going literally all the way back to the disciples and to Christ himself. This is called apostolic succession.

Protestants cannot confess this due to breaking away from the church in the sixteenth century and refusing to submit to its authority. Arguably, the breakaway in part grew from an earnest desire to correct abuse in the church, which has always existed in the church and every church today as well as every organization, for fallible humans in need of redemption and grace comprise the church and all organizations. Therefore, the doctrine of

---

10. My church history professor in seminary wisely said that "all heresy is true. That is precisely why it is so dangerous. It is dangerous because it contains an element of truth." It is, however, not wholly true and that it contains some truth is precisely why it can be so enticing to so many and dangerous. She also wisely said heresy never dies; it merely resurrects itself repeatedly and in new forms. This is a profound truth.

safeguarding and passing on the tradition is called apostolic succession and can only be claimed rightly by the Catholic Church and Orthodox today. It literally is an unbroken line passing on the tradition that goes all the way back to Christ. Notice the updated Nicene Creed originally penned in 325 CE at the Council of Nicene and later updated at the First Council of Constantinople in 381 CE that reads toward the very end, "We believe in one holy catholic and apostolic Church."[11] The only groups today that can claim they are truly apostolic in the sense they go all the way back to the apostles in an unbroken chain are truly the Roman Catholic Church and the Orthodox Churches of the East.

At the Council of Chalcedon in 451 when adopting the position regarding the two natures in one person of Christ, Pope Leo had written a letter to Flavian, the archbishop of Constantinople. It is known today as his famous *Tome of Leo*. The letter was read to the bishops at the ecumenical council. After it was read, the bishops at the council replied, *"Peter has spoken thus through Leo!"* This demonstrates the well-established office of the papacy at this time, although it can be seen already in that others had written that when disputes arise recourse or the jurisdiction that needs to be applied to is the Bishop of Rome, but it also demonstrates apostolic succession through the popes was understood. The current pope at that time, St. Leo, spoke through the authority and seat of Peter, who in the first century was given that authority from Jesus as recorded in Matthew 16:13–19, discussed in the next section. Therefore, in this instance apostolic succession is demonstrated through the Bishop of Rome, which passes on to the next Bishop of Rome until today. It just so happens this bishopric is the Holy See in which the seat of Peter resides.

Tradition along with this foundational premise of the church thus helps safeguard against bizarre, erroneous interpretations of Scripture and all other forms of heresy and falsehood. Otherwise, you will have opinion after opinion and disagreements and splinter churches who reject the authority of the church, which is

11. The much earlier Apostles' Creed toward the end reads, "I believe in the Holy Spirit, the holy catholic Church."

the case with Protestantism, with its hundreds of denominations. Protestantism, basically, is a refusal to submit to authority and presumption you know best in regards to truth, doctrine, and the proper, true interpretation of biblical texts—not the magisterium of the church, Christ's established church and guardian of the faith and tradition.[12]

12. See Bergsma, *Stunned by Scripture*, 120–21. Here one finds a true story the author articulates upon visiting a well-respected Protestant theologian. After listening to him for some time with some disconcertion, the author explained he piped up and said, "You have set yourself up as your own arbiter of truth!" The Protestant theologian replied, "Yes, well . . . that is the *Protestant principle*, isn't it?" Thus, one can rightly argue Protestants, especially the notion of *sola Scriptura*, sets up a situation where each individual decides what they think is best. However, one can rightly argue one always reads Scripture through a particular lens, usually the lens/theology of their faith community. Often these are arbitrary lenses that cherry pick texts to cohere to a particular theology. One should recall 2 Peter 1:20–21, noted in the text above, that implies Scripture is not subject to private interpretation. It thus needs a hierarchy to help establish its proper meaning, lest bizarre, erroneous interpretations prevail, which certainly is the case often with fallible human beings. Who better to offer the proper understanding than the church Christ instituted and intended to carry on his truth and ministry? It is carried on and passed on to generation after generation in an unbroken chain since Christ through the bishops. Many have argued that when one refuses to submit to authority and breaks away from the church, there will be no end to the fracturing of a breakaway group. This is precisely what one sees in the Protestant world today with the literally thousands of denominations that continue to pop up or split apart daily, all because of a refusal to submit to authority and a presumption that one knows what is right and that they or their group alone possess the truth and others do not. It is hard today to keep count of how many different types of Presbyterian churches there are. Furthermore, the splintering of Protestant demotions always seems to be at its core a split ultimately over the interpretation of Scripture. All will agree Scripture it authoritative, but how it is to be interpreted is at the core, usually whether in a strict literal sense or more in line with a less rigid spirit of the law sense. The latter realizing the complexity of how our texts were compiled and that the word of God is contained in the Bible but not in a literal sense in that every line or word of Scripture contains an infallible teaching or utterance of God. It holds a tension that Scripture comes to us mediated from its particular time and culture, not to mention we do not possess original documents of Scripture and scribal emendations are abundant. Usually the issues of homosexuality and other controversial topics conceal the real issue: how Scripture is to be interpreted. It can rightly be argued Scripture is always read through a particular tradition or lens even if one

Second Peter 1:20–21 reads: "First of all you must understand this, that no prophecy of scripture is a matter *of one's own interpretation*, because no prophecy ever came by human will, but men and women moved by the Holy Spirit spoke from God."[13] This makes apparent that the interpretation of Scripture is not a private matter to be decided upon individually or by a small group. Granted there is some leeway allowed in the interpretation of texts in the tradition and an understanding that texts of the Bible can be read on different levels: such as a historical/literal or a spiritual sense, including allegorical, moral/tropological, and anagogical (one should consult the *Catechism of the Catholic Church* [*CCC*,115–19]). Thomas Aquinas helpfully articulated these differing ways of reading the Bible; he espoused on these nicely in his *Summa Theologiae* and there are other, nuanced ways to categorize differing readings allowed by the Church. St. Augustine was helpful in articulating that the church is not as constrictive as one might surmise in regards interpreting biblical texts, especially when compared to how Protestants interpret them today, mostly via a plain sense or meaning of the text, which often causes problems. For example, these arise when explaining texts like the creation

---

thinks they have none but the Bible. Again, it needs to be reiterated, Scripture is always interpreted according to preconceived theological understandings, especially in evangelical churches today. Some readings are inappropriate; thus, Protestants do end up creating their own type of tradition that Scripture must be read through, although they likely have more wiggle room for private interpretation in Bible studies, provided they conform to the theology of the group they are a part of. Therefore, the differing protestant denominations can be conceived of as differing individual readings that become more normative for differing groups, though these denominations continue to have schism after schisms, usually not because of the issue of the authority of Scripture but rather the interpretation of Scripture. They are not guided by a magisterium that claims apostolic succession. One could argue Protestantism was founded on an individualism that smacks of ego and pride. However, that is not to criticize the millions of well-meaning and good Protestant brothers and sisters who still should properly be called Christian, for they still believe in Jesus and do share much in common with Catholics. Sometimes it is a matter of emphasis, though the two traditions share much in common, the paradox is there are also many differences as well.

13. I was reminded of Peter's words by Horn, *Why We're Catholic*, 80.

accounts in Genesis in light of what science has and continues to reveal. This is not a problem for Catholics but would have been for the second-generation reformer like John Calvin and those who still follow his views on Scripture even when they do not realize they are doing so today in the Protestant world.

The interpretation of Scripture is to be carefully and pastorally done through the teaching magisterium of the church, which Christ established, and is maintained through subsequent generations via apostolic succession. Now it will be see how Jesus founded his church upon Peter, the first pope. Church history then demonstrates how his authority was then passed to the successive bishops of Rome.

# Chapter II

# The Papacy

JESUS CLEARLY ESTABLISHES THE church and he does so by founding it upon the Apostle Peter, the rock.[1] In the Bible one learns it is instituted by God, founded upon Peter, who is given the keys to bind and loose in heaven and earth (Matt 16:13–20) and the apostles are given the power to forgive or retain sins (John 20:22–23), all of which is passed on to subsequent leaders

1. A common criticism of the church today, and with other religious institutions and traditions, particularly from those who classify themselves as spiritual and not religious, is that they are "man made." Those who claim to be spiritual and not religious are growing in number in our culture and they generally are not very knowledgeable about religion, much less the Bible, Christianity, and Catholicism. In response to this objection, it should be noted that the Catholic Church is not "man made," but rather, instituted by God and founded upon Peter who is given the keys to bound and loose in heaven and earth (Matt 16:13–20 ) and the apostles are given the power to forgive sins by God (John 20:22–23), all of which is passed on to subsequent leaders of the church until the Second Coming. Therefore, the argument the church is a "man-made" institution is not tenable, rather it is a convenient way to disregard truth and set oneself up as their own arbitrator of truth and in essence play God. America's past emphasis on rugged individualism and manifest destiny in the American dream regrettably lends itself to a type of autonomy that allows the ego to run amok and presume one knows best and what is right from wrong, along with an often robust disdain for others, particularly institutions, presuming arrogantly to possess the ability to know what is right or wrong. One even gleans this in our polarized political system. This is certainly not the case with all or most Americans and is a generalization. However, generalizations exist for a reason, for they contain an element of truth more often than not. On this issue, one need recall the insightful truth of St. Augustine when he said that ultimately "all sin is pride."

of the church until the second coming. The church thus is given the power to mediate God's forgiveness and the atoning work of Christ on the cross to people here on earth.

The absolute primacy and subsequent authority of Peter is seen in the Gospels and then the book of Acts. This is not in question. After all, he is the first disciple to be called, along with Andrew his brother, according to all four Gospels; he is also the disciple Jesus calls to walk on water to him on the Sea of Galilee (Matt 14:22–33). And according to John's Gospel, Peter is the one who is presented as having the chutzpah to cut off the ear of the servant of the Jewish high priest immediately following Jesus' arrest, as we are told he was carrying a sword (John 18:10–11; cf. Mark 14:47; Matt 26:51; Luke 22:50–51). In Luke, what then ensues of this act is that Jesus performs his final miracle of healing the high priest's servant, an act that demonstrates or presupposes a forgiveness of one's enemies, as he was there in an adversarial role to arrest Jesus.

When called, Peter along with Andrew, are told by Jesus that he will make them fishers of men (e.g., Matt 4:17; Mark 1:17). Peter stands out among the disciples and seems to have a strength to him, suggesting why he was picked to head the church. He possessed the fortitude, though God enabled him with this gift no doubt. How appropriate a remark by Jesus in expressing that he will make Peter a fisher of men for the soon-to-be head of the church he establishes and the first pope. It is therefore not a surprise Peter's strength and courage seem to be emphasized, with the exception of his denying Christ three times after his arrest. That in itself is full of lessons for Christians today. Again, one need recall when Jesus is arrested in the Garden of Gethsemane, it is Peter who cuts the ear off one of the temple guards trying to fight them off for his rabbi's sake.[2] That took great courage.

2. That Jesus predicted how Peter will die can be seen in John 21:18–19. That all the disciplines went to their deaths for the faith save one demonstrates their absolute certainty in Christ and the faith. After all, who would die for a lie? Most could have recounted and rejected the faith and have saved their lives. This suggests they believed the faith and Jesus rising from the dead and atoning for our sins were absolute truths for the disciples. And we know they were each firsthand witnesses to Christ. Many have argued this strongly attests

Not let us look at a pivotal text regrading Peter, the first pope, and the church Jesus founds upon him when the apostles are gathered together near Caesarea Philippi.

---

for the authenticity of the faith, including the Christian apologist Lee Strobel, *The Case for Christ*. Furthermore, that Jesus died for our sins according to the Scriptures, was raised from the dead, and appeared to his disciples afterward, and later five hundred people, was attested very early on in a creed recorded already before the gospels were written in one of Paul's letters (see 1 Cor 15:3–8). The Jewish historian Josephus, who never became Christian, astonishingly wrote with reverence regarding Jesus that he did surprising feats, was the Christ, was crucified and on the third day appeared. Thus, he attests to the resurrection and he is not even a Christian and this comes from a source outside the Bible but written very early and essentially contemporaneously with it. The text from the Jewish historian Josephus reads:

> About this time there lived Jesus, a wise man, if indeed one ought to call him a man. For he was one who performed surprising deeds and was a teacher of such people as accept the truth gladly. He won over many Jews and many of the Greeks. He was the Messiah. And when, upon the accusation of the principal men among us, Pilate had condemned him to a cross, those who had first come to love him did not cease. He appeared to them spending a third day restored to life, for the prophets of God had foretold these things and a thousand other marvels about him. And the tribe of the Christians, so called after him, has still to this day not disappeared. (*Jewish Antiquities*, 18.3.3 §63, Loeb Classical Library)

That Jesus was prophesized about in the Hebrew Scriptures is without question and exceeds this work. One need only see the amazing example of Second Isaiah for such (Isa 40–55). Perhaps its most famous text pointing to Christ reads:

> He was despised and rejected by others; a man of suffering and acquainted with infirmity; and as one from whom others hide their faces he was despised, and we held him of no account. Surely he has borne our infirmities and carried our diseases; yet we accounted him stricken, struck down by God, and afflicted. But he was wounded for our transgressions, crushed for our iniquities; upon him was the punishment that made us whole, and by his bruises we are healed. All we like sheep have gone astray; we have all turned to our own way, and the LORD has laid on him the iniquity of us all. He was oppressed, and he was afflicted, yet he did not open his mouth; like a lamb that is led to the slaughter, and like a sheep that before its shearers is silent, so he did not open his mouth." (Isa 53:3–7)

Now when Jesus came into the district of Caesarea Philippi, he asked his disciples, "Who do people say that the Son of Man is?" And they said, "Some say John the Baptist, but others Elijah, and still others Jeremiah or one of the prophets." He said to them, "But who do you say that I am?" Simon Peter answered, "You are the Messiah, the Son of the living God." And Jesus answered him, "Blessed are you, Simon son of Jonah! For flesh and blood has not revealed this to you, but my Father in heaven. And I tell you, you are Peter, and **on this rock** I will build my church, and the gates of Hades will not prevail against it. I will give you the keys of the kingdom of heaven, and whatever you bind on earth will be bound in heaven, and whatever you loose on earth will be loosed in heaven." (Matt 16:13–19)

Jesus is clearly playing off Peter's name, which means rock in Greek. Upon this rock clearly refers to Peter because he answered the question correctly and his name *Petros* means rock in Greek. Furthermore, Jesus appears to be talking to him in response to his immediate comment. That is the plain meaning of the text. Protestant attempts to explain this interpretation of the text are not tenable. They often argue or explain away such a blatantly clear understanding by suggesting Jesus in this text is not referring to Peter but rather a literal rock formation at the site that is argued was used for what has been termed pagan practice and sacrifice in the ancient world. Protestant arguments that Jesus was referring to that rock formation in the city of Caesarea Philippi are attempts to explain away that Peter was the first pope. To be fair, there is a large rock formation at the site, but this interpretation does not hold.[3] Clues for it do not exist in the text; besides, the

3. This interpretation is often advocated by Protestant evangelicals. I have actually been in Caesarea Philippi and had a lecture by a Protestant in which the presenter argued Jesus likely was pointing his hand toward the rock formation while speaking the words "on this rock I will build my church." One can also find this argument being presented on videos on Youtube filmed at Caesarea Philippi. One could argue a *double entendre* is advanced in the text in that both interpretations are correct. Though they can be harmonized, no clues in the text exist for the notion the rock formation where pagan practices

church in its role of safeguarding and passing on the tradition has always affirmed this text as referring to Peter being the rock upon which the church will be built and that Peter was the first pope. The Church affirms what Jesus explains after affirming Peter is the rock the church will be built on in this text, namely that he in his capacity as the first pope of the church will be given the "keys of the kingdom of heaven, and whatever you bind on earth will be bound in heaven, and whatever you loose on earth will be loosed in heaven" (v. 19). This interpretation is in fact suggested in the text by the play on his name and Jesus addressing him. This is the more literal reading of the text affirmed by the church.

---

occurred was intended and we certainly are not told Jesus was pointing to the rock formation in the text. This is not to deny that often biblical texts are multilayered and often have multiple meanings, just not in this case. The text is rather clear and explicit. Regarding multiple meanings of a text, one cannot help but think of the rabbinic analogy that suggests that at Sinai God's teaching or torah can be understood as coming down in the form of a beam of light that then goes into a prism atop the mountain. The light is then refracted into multiple lights going in different iterations. The different lights being refracted signify the different meanings and interpretations of Scripture. This is a helpful analogy, but certainly some interpretations can be erroneous and simply wrong. Thank goodness for the magisterium of the church which guides in the proper interpretations of texts and safeguards from strange, bizarre, and simply wrong readings of biblical texts. One could argue that since the time of Luther, the Protestant umbrella of Christianity has continued to fracture and fracture repeatedly over differing, subjective and often incorrect, and frankly sometimes bizarre, readings of biblical texts with no basis according to evidence or logic. By refusing to submit to authority and playing God in the sense that one presumes they have the proper interpretations of texts, one often errs in reading texts, including entire faith traditions. One could argue the problems today with the splintering of churches in Protestantism all started with Martin Luther's subjective readings of texts in which he thought he knew better than the church instituted by Christ to guard and pass on God's message. Recent works have questioned the mental stability of Luther. That he equated a bowel movement with salvation does in my view make him somewhat suspect, or crass to say the least. I have heard others say he was brilliant, and certainly a very prolific writer and teacher but that he also was very much a peasant and remained one to the end. Case in point: it has been documented when he had visitors over he would enjoy talking about flatulence at dinner and other subjects that most would find crude even in his day.

The Protestant suggestion is pure speculation and borders on polemical, suggesting the rock of paganism is what the church build itself atop of; it is suggesting an appropriation or supersessionism to some extent, that the church would grow atop and supplant the evil practices of the day. This is not altogether a bad notion, but it is just reading into the text something that is not there. It, however, is not a tenable interpretation, as it does not have evidence to back it. Besides, we are told in v. 13 that the event occurred in the district of Caesarea Philippi, so we do not know where exactly the disciples were located in the story of the text. Even if the rock formation was in view of the disciples, which is doubtful, when this story occurred, we do not know if it existed as it does now, as trees might have covered it back then. Furthermore, we are not told if the group was even in the city proper when the events recorded occurred; by mentioning the district and not the city, one must wonder if they were actually on the outskirts of the city itself instead of in it where the rock formation seems to be located. This further hurts the case that Peter is not intended as the rock in this text. Ultimately, it is clear he is and that Jesus explains upon him the church will be built. History then goes on to show this to be the case. All the early church documents, as well as all of its later documents, concur Peter became the first Bishop of Rome. This alone proves the Catholic view of the text to be true, as a fulfillment of Jesus' prophecy if you will.

Verse 19 intimates or subtly presupposes the important doctrine of apostolic succession, something only the Catholic Church can claim, an unbroken line passing on the tradition that goes all the way back to Christ. As noted above, church history then demonstrates how his authority was then passed on to succeeding bishops of Rome; it is illogical to think Christ would create a church and then have it die out after Peter. This point is widely reflected in the writings of the church fathers.[4] Thus, Clement becomes the next pope and so on up until Pope Francis today who now sits on Peter's throne in Rome. That the disciples are also given authority, particularly in matters of forgiving and retaining sins according to

4. See Bergsma, *Stunned by Scripture*, 35.

the Gospel of John that also is to be understood as being passed on to subsequent generations will be seen in what follows below under the section on the sacraments and reconciliation. A brief comment on papal infallibility is in order, a sorely misunderstood doctrine among Protestants. Protestants generally, and even some Catholics, do not understand the doctrine of papal infallibility. It only refers to official pronouncements or teachings done in his official teaching duty of his seat. This occurs when the pope acts *ex cathedra* (from the Chair of Peter). Surprisingly for many, the last official papal infallibility teaching technically goes all the way back to the 1950s by Pope Pius IX in defining the Immaculate Conception.[5] Such instances are indeed very rare.

5. Some have argued *Humanae Vitae* was infallible, but technically, it was not. The doctrine of papal infallibility was only affirmed at Vatican I in 1870. My friend William R. Cook reminded me of these points. One should see his *Francis of Assisi: The Way of Poverty and Humility* and his erudite video series in the Great Courses series, entitled *The Catholic Church: A History*.

Chapter III

# Purgatory

MOST DO NOT REALIZE that even Martin Luther believed in purgatory[1] and really even the Eucharist in the Catholic sense. His gripe was more with abuse in the church, which included indulgences, which is still not rightly understood today among even many Catholics. Technically, the Church never sold indulgences as most Protestants maintain, but that is a different discussion altogether. The topic at hand, purgatory, is actually a wonderful, reassuring doctrine. A priest once said our worst day in purgatory will be like our best day on earth. As noted above, one of the books missing in the limited Protestant canon is 2 Maccabees, which presupposes purgatory. Regrading Judas Maccabeus, 2 Maccabees 12:45 reads, "He made atonement for the dead, that they might be delivered from their sin."[2] This presupposes purgatory.

The logic of the doctrine presupposes a truth: We must be holy to see and be with God, thus purged even though your outcome of being with God has been resolved because of the atonement of Christ. As Christ has atoned for us already, we therefore do not die with mortal sins on us. Our venial sins are purged during our time in purgatory. It will be addressed further when examining the sacrament of reconciliation, but one need recall at this juncture that a clear distinction exists in the Bible in terms of sin, mortal and venial. First John 5:17 reads, "All wrongdoing is

1. Madrid, *Why We're Catholic*, 147.

2. This translation was taken form Horn, *Case for Catholicism*, 266. It is virtually the exact same as the NRSV translation.

sin, but there is sin that is not mortal." Mortal, grave sins bearing on one's eternal well-being that need to be atoned for by Christ and addressed through the sacrament of reconciliation are addressed in such texts as Gal 5:19–21, Rom 1:28–32, and others. Consequently, according to the Bible, there is no doubt that a hierarchy of sins and distinction between mortal and venial sins exits. This distinction will be addressed again when discussing the sacrament of reconciliation below. Thus, we must be purified and purged before coming into God's presence. Purgatory is a time of purification that burns off or clears away venial sins to make one holy so one can enter the presence of God, which is pure holiness. The logic is rather sound; one must be holy to be in God's presence and purgatory is the means to make one holy prior to entry in such grandeur and holiness—the presence of God.

Revelation 21:27 along with its preceding context explains nothing that is unclean can enter heaven.[3] We must be purged of our sins; otherwise, we remain unclean and cannot enter heaven. Furthermore, it must be recalled that to some extent we still must make amends for our sins, and recall we all do sit in the judgment seat of Christ after this life. Hence, a time of purgation is necessary for most of us. However, this is not a scary thing but rather, a good, reassuring thing. The time we spend undergoing purification might, in fact, be outside of time and thus done in an instant, though a measure of time itself.[4] One can glean the problem with finite language and talking about things of God at this point. Conjecture as to the pragmatics of purgatory does come into play to some degree, as all language about God is inadequate and analogical and because the specifics of purgatory are not fleshed out in biblical texts. Recall toward the end of his life, Thomas Aquinas had some sort of vision and never wrote again. Afterward he said all that he had written was but straw. If one of the most prolific and brilliant writers of the faith said such, how much more insignificant are the writings of anyone, including the present writer, about

---

3. I was reminded of this text by Horn, *Case for Catholicism*, 263.

4. On Pope Benedict XVI suggesting such, see Horn, *Why We're Catholic*, 146–47.

the faith. Thus, the doctrine of purgatory is biblical and the early church believed it, as the writings of the church fathers make apparent, such as those of Origen and Clement of Alexandria among others.[5] St. Augustine very early on in his famous *City of God* advanced the view quite clearly.[6]

Again, the logic is thus: we must be completely holy to see and be in the presence of God. Thus, purgatory finishes purging one of the venial sins, not mortal sins. This is not to deny a purging of venial sins also can occur and does occur in this life here on earth. We have all likely seen people undergoing such in this life, and how it helps when people offer up their suffering to Christ or join it to Christ's suffering, an act one finds in Catholicism, but not Protestantism.[7]

It need be remembered that one's ultimate salvation is not in question in regards to the doctrine of purgatory and one proceeding there after death: Christ already took care of that. Additionally, in regards to this beautiful doctrine, recall the Bible explains one can build up treasures in heaven (Matt 6:20) and a natural corollary follows that one can be purged here in this life reducing time in purification after this life.[8] This suggests what

5. Horn, *Case for Catholicism*, 273–76. Here one sees early on Clement of Alexandria, Origen, and Tertullian affirming the understanding of purgatory, thus revealing it was understood early on in the church and is not a later development. It is logical and follows from the Bible. It addresses the very important need to be purified before entering God's presence. These Fathers of the Church all write about such a need, which is consistent with the witness of Scripture. On p. 276 Horn writes, "The early historical witness, therefore, supports the antiquity of the Catholic doctrine of purgatory rather than the common Protestant position that the soul requires no purification or preparation after death." Clearly the Protestant view, as so often and ironically, is not consistent here with the witness of Scripture.

6. Horn, *Case for Catholicism*, 273.

7. This is usually done with recourse to or a view to Col 1:24, which reads, "I am now rejoicing in my sufferings for your sake, and in my flesh I am completing what is lacking in Christ's afflictions for the sake of his body, that is, the church."

8. Although time constraints preclude delving into the subject, indulgences granted in this life, such as a plenary indulgence, can do the same thing. It must be noted this is an often misunderstood concept and people should

we do on earth has consequences after this life and works matter, which will be addressed further below. It also needs to be noted that it is not necessarily the case the purification is painful. If it is, God is so gracious and never conforms to the box we all attempt to put God in it is therefore likely it is only but for an instant, and we also have then the assurance of eternal salvation after it, thus it is hardly a hardship. For if it is truly a dusk, the dawn will come and last for eternity.

Common sense tells us one who has lived a life of debauchery and hurting others, repents, and accepts Christ on his or her death will undoubtedly have a different purging experience than say a person who has lived a holy life and gone to Mass every day for the last thirty years of his or her life. This is logical and just. A St. Theresa of Avila or a Mother Teresa likely needs less purging, if any, than a person who lived his life as if God did not exist but comes into the faith on his/her death bed.[9] Thus, the logic is cogent and the Bible confirms we have some cleansing to do after death before entering heaven. It is required to make us holy to be with the Transcendent, Holy One. Purgatory is a sound doctrine affirmed through the ages in the Church, and one should take solace in it and not be afraid, for it prepares and heals us if you will. Other biblical texts presuppose it and a purification after death. Saint Paul talks about the purification upon the end of our lives:[10]

> The work of each builder will become visible, for the Day will disclose it, because it will be revealed with fire, and the fire will test what sort of work each has done.

---

consult a priest on the complicated matter.

9. It is interesting to read the saints of the church, as these exceedingly holy individuals all affirm their own sinfulness. They seem to be more aware of it in large measure due to their holiness and connection to God. They teach us that if they are sinful, then we must bear in mind we all are and fall short of the glory of God (Rom 3:23). Thus, if some of the saints go to purgatory, perhaps we all do for a period. Again, speculation comes into play here, as only God knows precisely how things go down upon death and our purification functions before our eternity with God.

10. Horn, *Why We're Catholic*, 148. Horn also reminded me of this text and cites it here.

If what has been built on the foundation survives, the builder will receive a reward. If the work is burned up, the builder will suffer loss; the builder will be saved, but only as through fire. (1 Cor 3:13–15)

Chapter IV

# The Real Presence of Christ
# in the Eucharist

VATICAN II DECLARED THE Eucharist to be "the source and summit of the Christian life" (See *Catechism of the Catholic Church*,
no. 1324; *Lumen Gentium*, no. 11). Catholics are a Eucharistic
people (Pope Benedict XVI) and if one does not believe in the
real presence of Christ in the Eucharist, one is not a Catholic.[1] The
Eucharist is the summit of the faith and really the culmination and
main reason for the Mass, albeit the liturgy of the Word that pre-
cedes it in the Mass is important as well. Some argue the center of
the Mass is the Eucharist while the center of a Protestant church
service is the sermon, the proclamation of the Word.[2] Jesus the
Christ himself instituted the summit of the Christian faith.

Ultimately, the Eucharist is a profound mystery of the faith
and we accept it on faith, namely we accept on faith that the bread
and wine of the Eucharist become the literal body, blood, soul, and
divinity of Christ in the host at the Mass after the priest offers the

1. This latter point was told to me by my friend Father Bill Collins of San
Antonio.

2. The present author had a professor in seminary suggest this. I am reminded of the theology of Karl Barth here and his threefold form of the word
in which he conceptualized the revelation of the word or Jesus as being three
concentric circles. He said the word of God is revealed, written, and proclaimed. Revealed in Jesus, written in the Bible, and proclaimed in the pulpit. I
would argue he missed one. I would argue the Word or *Logos* (See John 1:1) is
revealed in Jesus, is taken into us in the Eucharist, is written in Scripture, and
is proclaimed in the pulpit.

words of consecration and lays his hands over the elements. This transformation of the bread and wine into the real presence of Christ is known as transubstantiation. This process brings about the real presence of Christ in the Eucharist and it is believed to be the real presence of Christ because Jesus explains it is in the New Testament. The real presence of Christ in the Eucharist was believed from the very beginning of the church up to the present.[3] It is therefore most appropriate that during the Mass after the liturgy of the Word during the liturgy of the Eucharist immediately following the words of consecration the priest says, "The mystery of the faith." For it is truly a mystery and perhaps one of the hardest ones to grasp of the divine mysteries, but the foundational one that must be accepted on faith for Catholics. As it is a mystery, to some extent a complete understanding and grasp of it, especially seeing we make use of finite language and finite minds, will elude us this

3. A friend reminded me the other day of a frequent objection or perhaps comment he receives from Protestants regarding the real presence of Christ in the Eucharist. Protestants often comment that if you really believed in the real presence, then why does not every Catholic prostrate themselves before the elements in absolute reverence? There is a valid point here. After all, if we Catholics really believe in the real presence, why are we not being more reverent before it and partaking of it daily? Undoubtedly, there are many reasons why, such as our busy schedules and simply our laziness, but perhaps and regrettably also in part due to an element of doubt for some of us as to the real presence. It is true if it really is what Jesus and the Church say it is we all need to pay the Eucharist more reverence, partake of it more, and partake of it more worthily. That is, most of us likely need to go to reconciliation before partaking of it. Having said that, one only needs to go to reconciliation prior to taking the Eucharist if one has committed or has mortal sins on their souls or conscience. If one only has venal sins, it is perfectly acceptable to take the Eucharist at Mass. One wonders what percentage on any given Sunday should really be refraining from it until they have gone to the sacrament of reconciliation. Only God knows and we should not judge, but suffice it to say it is highly likely seeing we are all fallible creatures that many need partake of the Eucharist more reverently. Recall Pope Francis said the church is a field hospital for the sick. How true a sentiment. And recall the words of Jesus: When Jesus heard this, he said to them, "Those who are well have no need of a physician, but those who are sick; I have come to call not the righteous but sinners" (Mark 2:17; cf. Matt 9:12; Luke 5:31–31). The Eucharist is the healing balm and medicine we all need for our spiritual ills.

side of heaven. It is, hence, truly a mystery that Christ instituted and the Church has always affirmed.

Ample evidence for the belief of the real presence of Christ in the Eucharist from the very beginning recorded in the New Testament and then afterward in the Church exists. These can especially be seen in documents written right after those of the New Testament.[4] The first-century Christian document, the *Didache*, clearly understands the real presence of Christ in the Eucharist. Of this document it is written that it "confirms what the Church had always thought, namely, that the Real Presence was the uniform belief of ancient Christianity."[5] The "early Church Fathers uniformly affirmed the Real Presence of Christ's body and blood."[6] We today still do use, perhaps regrettably, medieval language to explain transubstantiation[7] and accidents, the technical language used to explain how the bread and wine becomes the real presence, and some have intimated it is outdated, but it is still an objective truth nonetheless. It is perhaps best left to theologians to flesh out better, updated parlance to explain the phenomenon and truth so fundamental to the faith. A difficult task no doubt, but an important one.

Interestingly, and I would argue providentially, Jesus was born in Bethlehem, though he was from Nazareth in the north in Galilee. In Hebrew, Bethlehem literally translates house (*beth*) of bread (*lhem*). Recall the prophecy in the Hebrew Scriptures that the Savior, the ruler of Israel whose origins are of old, ancient times would come from Bethlehem (Micah 5:1–4a); thus, Jesus being born in or coming into the world in this locale is first a fulfillment of the Scriptures. *Beth* or more accurately in Hebrew *Bet* can also mean temple, so one could say Bethlehem means "temple of

---

4. See both O'Conner, *Hidden Manna*, and Howell, *Eucharist for Beginners*.

5. Howell, *Eucharist for Beginners*, 54.

6. Howell, *Eucharist for Beginners*, 53.

7. This notion was suggested in private conversations with medieval historian William R. Cook. As noted above, transubstantiation is the technical term for the bread and wine at Mass becoming the literal body and blood of Christ, thus his real presence: body, blood, soul, and divinity in the elements of the bread and wine, in spite of our senses not being able to perceive them.

bread." It is interesting that in Hebrew the city name is always broken into two words and not one (תיב םחל). In the past some have said that the city likely produced a large amount of bread, which gave it its name, though there is no evidence for this and every city/household would have produced their own bread. Thus, it is unlikely the name derives from being a bread manufacturing city in ancient times. Another suggestion scholars have made was that it once was a city in which a god by the name of *Lhem* was venerated and his temple stood in the city, hence temple or *bet* of *Lhem*. The problem with this interpretation is such a god is not attested anywhere in antiquity and one would expect his name to appear in Canaanite texts such as those found at Ugarit in modern-day Syria. Several Canaanite deities are attested at the site; curiously, there is no reference to a *Lhem*. Furthermore, no evidence for a temple at the location in the West Bank has been found, albeit hardly any archeological digs have occurred in Bethlehem.

In view of Jesus explicitly stating he is the bread of life (John 6:35, 48, 51) and that his real presence appears in the Eucharist celebrated daily and venerated at Adoration, perhaps it is by God's providential design that the bread of life, Jesus, was born in a place that can be literally translated as the temple of bread or the house of bread. Jesus thus came from the house of bread and is the very bread of life himself. He is portrayed as the new temple in the gospels and he is the temple of bread in a very literal way if you will. In light of Jesus being the bread of life and his institution of the Eucharist at the Last Supper, and most notably what one reads in John 6, in which Jesus frequently insists upon his being the bread of life,[8] it is perhaps best to say Jesus, the bread of life, comes from

8. John 6:33–42 reads: "For the bread of God is that which comes down from heaven and gives life to the world." They said to him, "Sir, give us this bread always." Jesus said to them, "I am the bread of life. Whoever comes to me will never be hungry, and whoever believes in me will never be thirsty. But I said to you that you have seen me and yet do not believe. Everything that the Father gives me will come to me, and anyone who comes to me I will never drive away; for I have come down from heaven, not to do my own will, but the will of him who sent me. And this is the will of him who sent me, that I should lose nothing of all that he has given me, but raise it up on the last day. This is indeed the will of my Father, that all who see the Son and believe in him may

the city called house or temple of bread. Jesus explicably explains in John 6:35 and again in v. 48: "I am the bread of life" (cf. John 6:41).[9] Thus, though we do not know why the city originally was called Bethlehem and no scholarly suggestions adequately account for the origins of the locale's name, I would suggest it was part of God's providential design, for the Bread of Life came from the house/temple of bread, and this also a fulfillment of prophecy for the coming of the messiah (Micah 5:2).

Jesus certainly is the new Temple (or *Bet*) for Christians. The institution of the Eucharist can be seen in the text of the Last Supper in Luke 22:14–20:

> When the hour came, he took his place at the table, and the apostles with him. He said to them, "I have eagerly desired to eat this Passover with you before I suffer; for I tell you, I will not eat it until it is fulfilled in the kingdom of God." Then he took a cup, and after giving thanks he said, "Take this and divide it among yourselves; for I tell you that from now on I will not drink of the fruit of the vine until the kingdom of God comes." Then he took a

---

have eternal life; and I will raise them up on the last day." Then the Jews began to complain about him because he said, "I am the bread that came down from heaven." They were saying, "Is not this Jesus, the son of Joseph, whose father and mother we know? How can he now say, 'I have come down from heaven'?"

9. This is one of Jesus' seven "I am" statements he makes in the Gospel of John. These are highly significant, for they are divinity claims, as God explains to Moses in Exod 3:14, "I am who I am." God also reveals to Moses his divine name Yahweh, which likely derives from the verb "to be." So, when Jesus says, "I am the bread of life," he is playing off the divine name and revealing or saying he is God. He is saying I am God and the bread of life. It is interesting to note that he makes seven of these "I am" claims, which itself is significant, as seven in antiquity was a number signifying wholeness or completeness, as in the seven days of creation. It is furthermore noteworthy that of the seven different "I am" claims Jesus makes, the most frequent of all of them have to do with him being the bread of life (6:35, 48, 51). Mark 14:62 also has Jesus saying, "I am" (*ego eimi*), but most scholars only see "I am" divinity claims by Jesus in John's Gospel. It is no wonder after he makes one such claim, one reads that the Jews were so enraged they wanted to kill him, as they believed he was committing blasphemy. John 8:58–59 reads, "Jesus said to them, 'Very truly, I tell you, before Abraham was, I am.' So they picked up stones to throw at him, but Jesus hid himself and went out of the temple."

loaf of bread, and when he had given thanks, he broke it and gave it to them, saying, "This is my body, which is given for you. Do this in remembrance of me." And he did the same with the cup after supper, saying, "This cup that is poured out for you is the new covenant in my blood." (cf. Matt 26:26–29; Mark 14:22–25)

Notice Jesus never suggests he means things in a symbolic manner. He is instituting a new covenant, which was predicted by the prophet Jeremiah (see Jer 31:31–34), and commanding his followers to partake in his body and blood that is poured out for his followers.

John 6 offers the most striking words of Jesus revealing the Real Presence in the Eucharist. He shockingly claims, "Unless you eat my flesh and drink my blood, you have no life in you" (John 6:53). Undoubtedly, this was a violation of torah (Lev 17:14), but God created torah and Jesus' call to violate it by drinking his blood presupposed he is God, for only God can change torah. The classic and correct response/argument that he does not mean what he says in a purely symbolic sense, what Protestants often contend is demonstrated by what occurs next in the text of John. Upon Jesus' providing this hard teaching that violates torah, and people walking away, Jesus does not say, "Oh, no, wait a second, I mean it symbolically." He allows the people to leave. Thus, it is meant literally and this has been the classic Catholic response among apologetics, which is logical and sound. Again, this presupposes the divinity[10] of Christ because who could outright reject or con-

---

10. The divinity of Christ is clearly presupposed in this work and a prerequisite to the Christian faith. Hundreds of works through the ages address the topic, starting with the Bible itself. If one is looking for a modern-day helpful treatment on the subject, the apologetic work noted above already of Lee Strobel, entitled *A Case for Christ*, is most helpful. One of his many cogent arguments for the divinity of Christ, which the present author would argue is demonstrated subtly and not so subtly on virtually every page of the gospels, is done by way of asking who would claim to be God unless they were a lunatic or who they claimed to be. We know Jesus was not a mad man. This line of reasoning was actually much older than Strobel's work. It was argued about one hundred years before his work among German scholars, the world's most prolific biblical scholars.

tradict torah in first-century Palestine but God himself? The pertinent text of John 6 reads:

> [47] "Very truly, I tell you, whoever believes has eternal life. [48] *I am the bread of life.* [49] Your ancestors ate the manna in the wilderness, and they died. [50] This is the bread that comes down from heaven, so that one may eat of it and not die. [51] I am the living bread that came down from heaven. Whoever eats of this bread will live forever; and the bread that I will give for the life of the world is my flesh." [52] The Jews then disputed among themselves, saying, "How can this man give us his flesh to eat?" [53] So Jesus said to them, "*Very truly, I tell you, unless you eat the flesh of the Son of Man and drink his blood, you have no life in you.* [54] Those who eat my flesh and drink my blood have eternal life, and I will raise them up on the last day; [55] for my flesh is true food and my blood is true drink. [56] Those who eat my flesh and drink my blood abide in me, and I in them. [57] Just as the living Father sent me, and I live because of the Father, so whoever eats me will live because of me. [58] This is the bread that came down from heaven, not like that which your ancestors ate, and they died. But the one who eats this bread will live forever." [59] He said these things while he was teaching in the synagogue at Capernaum. [60] When many of his disciples heard it, they said, "This teaching is difficult; who can accept it?" [61] But Jesus, being aware that his disciples were complaining about it, said to them, "Does this offend you? [62] Then what if you were to see the Son of Man ascending to where he was before? [63] It is the spirit that gives life; the flesh is useless. The words that I have spoken to you are spirit and life. [64] But among you there are some who do not believe." For Jesus knew from the first who were the ones that did not believe, and who was the one that would betray him. [65] And he said, "For this reason I have told you that no one can come to me unless it is granted by the Father." [66] Because of this many of his disciples turned back and no longer went about with him. [67] So Jesus asked the twelve, "Do you also wish to go away?" [68] Simon Peter answered him, "Lord, to whom can we go? You have the words of eternal life. [69] We have

come to believe and know that you are the Holy One of God." [70] Jesus answered them, "Did I not choose you, the twelve? Yet one of you is a devil." [71] He was speaking of Judas son of Simon Iscariot, for he, though one of the twelve, was going to betray him. (John 6:47–71)

Jesus' command to eat his flesh and drink his blood is striking and would have been all the more so to an ancient audience, especially a Jewish one since it violates God's commandments.[11] The ancient Hebrews believed the life force (*nephesh*) was in the blood (*dam*). Leviticus 17:11 reads, "For the life of the flesh is in the blood; and I have given it to you for making atonement for your lives on the altar; for, as life, it is the blood that makes atonement." Since the *Nephesh* is in the *dam*, in a very real, literal way when we drink the wine, as well as eat his flesh in the bread, we are partaking in the very life force of Christ. And he tells us we must eat his flesh and drink his blood or there is no life in us (John 6:53). That the life-force is in the blood is timeless truth, as a blood workup and panel tells a doctor today everything about what is going on in one's body. It transports everything for a person, even oxygen, or the breath as an ancient would understand it; thus, the *dam* or blood is the very essence of life for a person today. It is a person's true life-force as the Hebrew Scriptures or

11. I have come across another line of interpretation Protestants make to address John 6 and explain away its pointing to the Eucharist. However, no scholar takes it seriously. The argument is that John was writing his gospel at Ephesus and possibly first addressing its inhabitants, as later documents seem to suggest he was there with Mary. Archeology has shown there was a cult of the god Dionysus (one of the dying and rising gods of antiquity that follows the agriculture cycle) at the site. It is thought that during an annual festival people went into the god's temple and feasted on meat dedicated to the god and allowed the blood of the meat to drip down their face. Thus, the evangelist was saying or intimating that one need not eat the flesh dedicated to Dionysus but that of the true god, Jesus. One issue with this line of thought is that the cult of Dionysus was ubiquitous in antiquity and virtually no scholars think there was an attempt to say on the part of the gospel writers that one greater than Dionysus is here in Jesus. Though this is true, clues are lacking in our texts for such a polemic and so with understanding John 6 as suggesting a polemic against the god in favor of Jesus. This is yet another unsuccessful attempt to explain away the reference to the Eucharist in John 6, a most pivotal text.

Torah explains. Doctors today would undoubtedly concur. Recall the words of Hebrews 9:22 in the New Testament: "Indeed, under the law almost everything is purified with blood, and without the shedding of blood there is no forgiveness of sins." The last clause provides an answer for the atonement, why Jesus had to die on the cross the way he did.

An interesting and often missed reference Jesus makes to the Eucharist can be seen in the Gospels of Matthew and Luke. In the Lord's Prayer, Jesus demonstrates and teaches us how to pray to his father: "Give us this bread our daily bread" (Matt 6:11; Luke 11:3). It is not very well known that there is uncertainty in regards to the specific translation of the Greek term rendered in English as "daily." There is likely more than meets the eye in the choice of this word. The Greek word in question—*epousion*—is derived from a root word of uncertain meaning. The root seems to have a definition of "for today, for the coming day or necessary for existence." It is probable that the term has other connotations, such as that of "extraordinary, super-long lasting or supernatural." Thus, some have argued, such as St. Jerome, that instead of "daily bread," a rendering of "super-substantial bread" is the better translation of Jesus' word in our beloved prayer.

The word Jesus used, which is most often translated into English as "daily," is not widely attested; in fact, it only occurs in two instances in the entire New Testament, in Matthew 6:11 and Luke 11:3. Thus, the exact and most appropriate translation is ambiguous. The term might simply mean "daily" or "for tomorrow" or it may suggest a supernatural type of bread. How one interprets this has big implications. If the author intended a "supernatural bread," it would be more in line with a Catholic view of the Eucharist and the doctrine of transubstantiation. Therefore, one would more likely understand this particular word as foreshadowing and pointing to the importance of the Eucharist. This possibility in the Lord's Prayer remains open and must be considered as a possibility.

When turning to Pauline literature, it is important to note what St. Paul says about the Eucharist. First Corinthians 10:15–17 reads:

> I speak as to sensible people; judge for yourselves what I say. The cup of blessing that we bless, is it not a sharing in the blood of Christ? The bread that we break, is it not a sharing in the body of Christ? Because there is one bread, we who are many are one body, for we all partake of the one bread.

Paul understands the cup as the blood of Christ. In no way is it implied or suggested to be so in a symbolic sense, nor would the church ever think such until those who broke away from the church Christ established well over a thousand years later. That it even unites us is amazing. Later in the same letter Paul writes:

> Whoever, therefore, eats the bread or drinks the cup of the Lord in an unworthy manner will be answerable for the body and blood of the Lord. Examine yourselves, and only then eat of the bread and drink of the cup. For all who eat and drink without discerning the body, eat and drink judgment against themselves. (1 Cor 11:27–29)

The Apostle to the Gentiles would not have penned this had he not understood the real presence of Christ in the Eucharist!

As noted above, it needs to be reiterated that "not only do New Testament Scriptures identity the Eucharist as Jesus' actual Body and Blood, but the Fathers uniformly and unanimously confirm this."[12] And we have seen that the gospels, particularly John 6, as well as other New Testament texts such as those from the Apostle Paul, are very clear on this point. It is thus biblical, and the church since the beginning has understood this doctrine. It was not until later reformers of the Reformation started to get away from this idea. It is to be noted that Martin Luther's notion of the Eucharist was not all that different than the Catholic Church's. His issues were with other matters, which are touched on further below.

P. Madrid, citing St. Ignatius of Antioch's *Letter to the Smyrnaeans* 6:2—7:1, writes regarding the Eucharist:

> This was the faith of the earliest Christians, as testified to by leading figures of the young church, such as Saint

---

12. Bergsma, *Stunned by Scripture*, 88.

Ignatius of Antioch, who would be martyred around 107. He was a disciple of John the apostle and learned the doctrine of the Eucharist directly from him, an eyewitness to the Last Supper. "Take note," he said, "of those who hold heterodox opinions on the grace of Jesus Christ which has come to us, and see how contrary their opinions are to the mind of God. . . . They abstain from the Eucharist and from prayer because they do not confess that the Eucharist is the flesh of our savior Jesus Christ, flesh which suffered for our sins and which that Father, in his goodness, raised up again. They who deny the gift of God are perishing in their disputes."

These early Catholics, some of whom, like Ignatius of Antioch, knew the apostle personally, were adamant that the Eucharist they celebrated was not merely a symbol of Jesus, nor was it only a memorial meal.[13]

Assuredly, this passage can be rather frightening, especially its comment regarding those who deny the Eucharist as being the flesh of Christ. In regards to not accepting what the Eucharist is, one reads, "They who deny the gift of God are perishing in their disputes." One hopes that is too harsh. It is argued that Ignatius wrote this only six years after Paul penned the lines in 1 Corinthians 11:27,[14] that "whoever, therefore, eats the bread or drinks the cup of the Lord in an unworthy manner will be answerable for the body and blood of the Lord."

It should be stated at this juncture in an attempt to head off another objection that might arise for some in this discussion: the Mass does not re-sacrifice Christ, but it is a sacrifice offered to God recalling the ultimate sacrifice, and we then partake in it and in Christ, quite literally through taking in the real presence of Christ in the Eucharist.[15] It is here we join our sacrifice to Christ's.

13. Madrid, *Why Be Catholic*, 57–58.

14. Horn, *Why We're Catholic*, 114.

15. On the Eucharist being a type of sacrifice and fulfillment of Old Testament/Hebrew Bible prophecy, see Howell, *Eucharist for Beginners*, 43–65. For a helpful quote from one of the earliest Christian documents outside the New Testament, the first-century *Didache*, understanding the real presence of

It has been the consistent teaching of the Church that the Eucharist is to be understood as a sacrifice, from writings immediately following the disciples (Justin Martyr, Irenaeus), from the first-century *Didache*, to later prominent Catholic writers and councils such as that of Trent and popes affirming it such as John Paul II. Almost all, including the Council of Trent, affirm that is what was prophesied about already in one of the books of the twelve, in Malachi. Malachi 1:11 speaks of the how the Gentiles will offer "a pure offering in every place." In noting this, the Council of Trent also speaks of how Paul discussing the Eucharistic table to the Corinthians equates it with an altar, which presupposes or implies a sacrifice offered to God. Thus, the Eucharistic celebration can and should be understood as a sacrifice, among other things such as communion.[16] At the Mass:

> The Father's love for his Son Jesus extends to us too as he offers us the same sacrifice of his son in the Eucharist. We offer that same sacrifice back to the Father with the plea that he would accept us through his Son. We can be reconciled to God only through Christ's sacrifice. For this reason, our worship today must contain the same sacrifice if we are to continue to be acceptable to the Father.[17]

Without such a sacrifice we are not truly worshipping; thus, if the Eucharist sacrifice is not part of the service, one is not properly worshipping and acceptable to God. The implications of this for Protestant churches goes without being said, as they technically offer communion or a symbolic memorial, but not the actual Eucharist and real presence of Christ as the Mass does. Catholics and the Orthodox also require a valid ordained priest to offer the

---

Christ in the Eucharist as well as it being a sacrifice, see p. 54. The document speaks of the importance of Christians confessing their sins before taking the Eucharist, as is done today. It speaks of our sacrifice when we take the Eucharist. We are joining our sacrifice to or making a sacrifice to the one already made by Christ Jesus when we partake in the Eucharist.

16. Virtually all of this info on the Eucharist as a sacrifice and the references to it in early writings and the Council of Trent was taken from Howell, *Eucharist for Beginners*, 53–58.

17. Howell, *Eucharist for Beginners*, 58.

Eucharist; Protestant pastors are not considered valid ordained priests. This should give any Protestant pause.

There is a story regarding the Catholic author Flannery O'Connor overhearing at a party someone quote the later reformer Zwingli in regards to the Eucharist being a purely symbolic act. It is said her response was that if it is purely a symbolic act, then to hell with it. There is an element of truth to this anecdotal story. If it is symbolic, why bother with it. Obviously, as has been seen, it is not and that is why it is offered daily in the Catholic faith, as opposed to communion being offered monthly or even less in many Protestant churches.

Additionally, there is a substantial amount of evidence for Eucharistic miracles.[18] One should not dismiss these out of hand before learning more about them and hearing the countless stories surrounding the Blessed Sacrament, although they are not a requirement of the faith. I know of healing stories associated with

18. In talking with a colleague of mine who is a specialist in substance abuse and an expert on Alcoholics Anonymous, he explained the problem with addiction or addicts is that at their core there is a "spiritual malady." He explained this is explicitly stated to be the case in the Alcoholics Anonymous Book. He explained the only true way to healing from the grip of addictions comes from a religious experience and a true surrendering to God, along with working the steps daily such as prayer and Scripture reading, such as *Lectio Divina*, attending meetings and helping others. He explained one must completely surrendering to God. In light of his comments regarding the core, fundamental issue being a "spiritual malady," one cannot help but wonder if partaking in the Eucharist would not be immensely helping and healing, especially considering what it is one is parting in, the body, blood, soul, and divinity of Christ. As the Eucharist is understood to be a cleansing and healing of the soul among other things, it therefore stands to reason the Eucharist could be the precise medicine and healing balm needed to address the "spiritual malady" addicts regrettably have to suffer. That it is offered daily in the Church is a gift. Protestants do not offer communion daily, sometimes only once a month, because they do not understand the real presence of Christ in the elements as aforementioned. The Catholic Church also does not understand their communion services when offered as an actual Eucharistic sacrifice, for their clergy are not valid priests. This is not to deny other treatments also help addiction, such as family therapy, cognitive behavioral theory, eye movement desensitization and reprocessing therapy (EMDR), among many others. New therapies continue to be developed, but one wonders if what is really, truly needed is the Eucharist.

it. This makes sense seeing what it is, and it would make sense why the church offers Mass and the Eucharist daily. If Christ is really present, as we believe, why would we not want to see him and take him into us daily for our sustenance, soul and help in traversing what is often a difficult life many of us lead? Protestants often are amazed Mass is offered daily, as many think this too much. However, they do not have an understanding of the real presence and as noted above many denominations only offer communion once a month in their churches.

In regards to Eucharist miracles, there have been several in which the host turned literally into human flesh and blood. One recent one seems to match with the DNA of one that occurred years ago. Undoubtedly, this is rare. There is a famous one in which the bread turned into the literal living tissue from a heart with blood that was and is completely healthy and had not decayed, which should have only seconds after leaving the body. Amazingly, its white blood cells did not die. It was even shown to be of a blood type of a Middle Easterner (AB)! This miracle has baffled scientists.[19] It even converted the atheist cardiologist who examined the sample not knowing what it was originally. He instantly observed the sample from the host was actually a very important, specific part of a heart he was well acquainted with.

I furthermore have had several of my students report to me that they feel a heaviness in the air when they go to Adoration, where the Blessed Sacrament is venerated outside of the Mass, thus where the real presence of Christ actually is before one tangibly. A friend recounted to me a feeling of immense holiness when visiting an adoration chapel the other day. He recounted to a me a mini-miracle in which he ran into an old priest/friend he had not seen in years, relaying the chances for such were unlikely and thus it was an instance of divine providence before the real presence of Christ.

19. Madrid, *Why Be Catholic*, 70 with citation.

Chapter V

# The Virgin Mary & the Saints

WITHOUT MARY, THERE IS no Jesus. She was chosen by God to be the mother of God (*theotokos*), and this is indeed no small matter.[1] Is there a bigger grace, honor, or favor that can be bestowed on a human being? Her veneration is completely warranted, appropriate, and biblical. Contrary to what many Protestants argue, Mary is not worshipped but rather honored. This distinction needs to be understood. It is not worshipping her in the Protestant sense or understanding; she is rather what should be conceptualized as honored or venerated. Terminology is important here. She is venerated, but one need know what that means and entails, as she is not worshipped as a god, but implored for her prayers and intercession before Jesus and the Triune God. She does her job in pointing and bringing others to her Son. She always points to Jesus in Scripture, and even in her later, more recent apparitions.

She thus points and brings devoted individuals to her son, always a facilitator or gentle being imploring others to go to her son. That is, Mary takes people to her son; she guides them to Christ and makes them closer to him. I know people who have told me their way to Christ is through his mother, Mary, and what a beautiful thing that is. In Catholic thought then, she always brings

1. For an excellent apologetic work for the Blessed Mother, see ch. 15, entitled "The Blessed Virgin Mary, Mother of God," in Horn, *Case for Catholicism*, 300–18. The following chapter cogently addresses the Immaculate Conception and Bodily Assumption of Mary. Time constraints preclude delving into these important doctrines of the faith here.

people to her son. Her apparitions, touched on below, in addition to pointing to Christ, frequently have a comforting message in which she expresses the need for people not to be afraid, which indeed is incredibly comforting, especially in our chaotic world that seems so divided, a division that is contrary to God and God's desire. This seems to be the case in what the Virgin of Guadalupe, the particular manifestation of the Blessed Virgin to the people of what is today Mexico,[2] said to Juan Diego.

When Catholics pray to her, especially in the Rosary, she is but asked to intercede for us as we do any member of the body of Christ, those alive today as well as those passed on, the latter being more common among Catholics. Recall the Rosary reads, "Pray for us sinners now and at the hour of our death, Amen." The body of Christ includes those both alive now and those who have passed on but are still alive. We are simply asking for her prayers and intercession before God. Who better to ask then the one we are told is "full of grace"[3] and honored by God? She is portrayed in the Bible as being the most holy after Jesus. After all, she is special because she was the mother of God who always points to Jesus, so who better to ask for intercession from.

Most Protestants do not realize the beautiful and wonderful prayer of the Rosary is amazingly biblical. It begins with, "Hail Mary full of grace," which is a direct quote form Luke 1:28. Luke 1:28 continues and reads regarding the angel coming to Mary: "And he came to her and said, 'Greetings, favored one! The Lord is with you.'" This can be translated "Hail Mary full of Grace [*hesed* in Hebrew] the Lord is with you!" That the angel exclaimed this to Mary is profound: where else in the Bible does an angelic being heap praise on a human? No wonder the church later declared her

2. That the Blessed Virgin manifests herself slightly differently in different contexts and times in her apparitions should come as no surprise, as she presents to people in a garb and appearance that particular people and times can relate to. It should be stated here that belief in Marian apparitions are not a requirement of the faith. However, if one really delves into them, it is exceedingly hard to dismiss the evidence, particularly her appearances in Cairo (Zeitoun) and Fatima.

3. Luke 1:28.

without sin and her Immaculate Conception. One does need stop and ponder how immensely amazing it is for a human to be told, "The Lord is with you." This presupposes her holiness, sacredness, and special status as a person. No wonder she was chosen to be the mother of God.

Later in Luke chapter 1 when her cousin Elizabeth encounters her outside of Jerusalem, she "exclaimed with a loud cry, 'Blessed are you among women, and blessed is the fruit of your womb'" (Luke 1:42). This is another part of the Rosary, betraying how biblical the helpful prayer is. Notice later how Mary points to God, and humbly so:

> And Mary said, "My soul magnifies the Lord, and my spirit rejoices in God my Savior, for he has looked with favor on the lowliness of his servant. Surely, from now on all generations will call me blessed; for the Mighty One has done great things for me, and holy is his name." (Luke 1:46–49)

The text correctly and prophetically reads, "from now on all generations will call me blessed (Luke 1:48b). That these texts uplift Mary to this extent and the Rosary is very biblical likely will come to a surprise to many Protestants. Catholicism is through and through biblical, something ironically Protestants think is not the case. The text makes clear praise is due Mary, which makes sense seeing God chose her to bear the Son of God.

Again, notice in the prayer of the Rosary that Mary is petitioned to pray for us, not worshipped in her own right. She is implored for our intercession before God.

> Hail Mary, full of grace, the Lord is with you;
> blessed are you among women,
> and blessed is the fruit of your womb, Jesus.
> Holy Mary, Mother of God,
> pray for us sinners
> now and at the hour of our death.
> Amen.

It is important to read in context Mary's visitation by the angel Gabriel and her subsequent visit with Elizabeth, John the Baptist's mother, in its entirety. Luke 1:26–49 reads:

> In the sixth month the angel Gabriel was sent by God to a town in Galilee called Nazareth, to a virgin[4] engaged to a man whose name was Joseph, of the house of David. The virgin's name was Mary. And he came to her and said, "Greetings, favored one! The Lord is with you." But she was much perplexed by his words and pondered what sort of greeting this might be. The angel said to her, "Do not be afraid, Mary, for you have found favor with God. And now, you will conceive in your womb and bear a son, and you will name him Jesus. He will be great, and will be called the Son of the Most High, and the Lord God will give to him the throne of his ancestor David. He will reign over the house of Jacob forever, and of his kingdom there will be no end." Mary said to the angel, "How can this be, since I am a virgin?" The angel said to her, "The Holy Spirit will come upon you, and the power of the Most High will overshadow you; therefore the child to be born will be holy; he will be called Son of God. And now, your relative Elizabeth in her old age has also conceived a son; and this is the sixth month for her who was said to be barren. For nothing will be impossible with God." Then Mary said, "Here am I, the servant of the Lord; let it be with me according to your word." Then the angel departed from her. In those days Mary

4. In the past some scholars have argued Mary likely was not a virgin and that she is understood as such in the gospels due to a mistranslation/misreading of a prophecy found in the Hebrew Bible, as the term suggesting virginity in Hebrew could simply mean a "young girl" and not necessarily a virgin. Isaiah 7:14 reads, "Therefore the Lord himself will give you a sign. Look, the young woman is with child and shall bear a son, and shall name him Immanuel." Young woman in Hebrew can also be translated as virgin; both are appropriate. Tradition has always affirmed she was a virgin and the gospels suggest this much. Her perpetual virginity would later be affirmed by the church. Had she not been a virgin, it in reality would not change much in regards to theology, but attempts to say she was not really a virgin need to be examined for what lays behind them, often an attempt to discredit the Bible, which would discredit Catholicism. Not surprisingly, it has been Protestants in the past who have advanced the idea Mary was not a virgin.

set out and went with haste to a Judean town in the hill country, where she entered the house of Zechariah and greeted Elizabeth. When Elizabeth heard Mary's greeting, the child leaped in her womb. And Elizabeth was filled with the Holy Spirit and exclaimed with a loud cry, "Blessed are you among women, and blessed is the fruit of your womb. And why has this happened to me, that the mother of my Lord comes to me? For as soon as I heard the sound of your greeting, the child in my womb leaped for joy. And blessed is she who believed that there would be a fulfillment of what was spoken to her by the Lord." And Mary said, "My soul magnifies the Lord, and my spirit rejoices in God my Savior, for he has looked with favor on the lowliness of his servant. Surely, from now on all generations will *call me blessed*; for the Mighty One has done great things for me, and holy is his name."

I have spent a day in the city that remembers the encounter between Mary and Elizabeth, in Ein Karem, outside of Jerusalem. Notice what it says regarding Elizabeth and her greeting of Mary: "And Elizabeth was filled with the Holy Spirit and exclaimed with a loud cry, 'Blessed are you among women, and blessed is the fruit of your womb. And why has this happened to me, that the mother of my Lord comes to me?'" (vv. 42–43).

The Spirit makes this truth known to Elizabeth and we hear in the text the biblical words later used to begin the Rosary, the beautiful and powerful prayer traditionally understood as being given to Saint Dominic (ca. 1214) in a vision of her. Elizabeth immediately recognizes Mary as carrying her Lord and as the mother of god (*theotokos*). What a remarkable comment she utters, no doubt a peculiar one for anyone to have overheard at the time especially in light of their already knowing each other and being related, for she utters in v. 43, "And why has this happened to me, that the mother of my Lord comes to me?"

It also is the case that many see the Blessed Virgin Mary portrayed in Revelation 12. The text is steeped in symbolism and one cannot help but see Mary in the apocalyptic text. The text reads:

A great portent appeared in heaven: a woman clothed with the sun, with the moon under her feet, and on her head a crown of twelve stars. She was pregnant and was crying out in birth pangs, in the agony of giving birth. Then another portent appeared in heaven: a great red dragon, with seven heads and ten horns, and seven diadems on his heads. His tail swept down a third of the stars of heaven and threw them to the earth. Then the dragon stood before the woman who was about to bear a child, so that he might devour her child as soon as it was born. And she gave birth to a son, a male child, who is to rule all the nations with a rod of iron. But her child was snatched away and taken to God and to his throne; and the woman fled into the wilderness, where she has a place prepared by God, so that there she can be nourished for one thousand two hundred sixty days. And war broke out in heaven; Michael and his angels fought against the dragon. The dragon and his angels fought back, but they were defeated, and there was no longer any place for them in heaven. The great dragon was thrown down, that ancient serpent, who is called the Devil and Satan, the deceiver of the whole world—he was thrown down to the earth, and his angels were thrown down with him. Then I heard a loud voice in heaven, proclaiming, "Now have come the salvation and the power and the kingdom of our God and the authority of his Messiah, for the accuser of our comrades has been thrown down, who accuses them day and night before our God. But they have conquered him by the blood of the Lamb and by the word of their testimony, for they did not cling to life even in the face of death. Rejoice then, you heavens and those who dwell in them! But woe to the earth and the sea, for the devil has come down to you with great wrath, because he knows that his time is short!" So when the dragon saw that he had been thrown down to the earth, he pursued the woman who had given birth to the male child. But the woman was given the two wings of the great eagle, so that she could fly from the serpent into the wilderness, to her place where she is nourished for a time, and times, and half a time. Then from his mouth the serpent poured water like a river after the woman, to sweep her away with the flood. But the earth came to the help of the woman; it opened its mouth and swallowed the river that the dragon had poured from his mouth. Then the dragon was angry with the woman, and went off to make war on the rest of her children, those who keep the commandments of God and hold the testimony of Jesus. (Rev 12:1–17)

It is interesting to see the chapter's concluding line explains the dragon being angry with the woman and how it went off to wage war on the rest of her children, the ones the texts says keep the "commandments of God and hold the testimony of Jesus." Several church fathers as well as popes have affirmed this interpretation, including John Paul II.[5] It is hard not to understand Mary in at least vv. 1–2.[6]

It must be noted that many wisely make a comparison between Mary and the ark of the covenant. Just as the ark carried God's Word (*debar* in Hebrew), so too Mary carried in her womb the word (*logos* in Greek) of God. The ark prefigured Mary, the one who would carry the word that was with God in the beginning and was God (John 1:1) that all things came into being through (John 1:3).

At this juncture it is most appropriate to remind the reader of the biblical concept mentioned above of the body of Christ, namely that we are all members of one body in Christ Jesus (Rom 12:4–5). And we all serve a different purpose and part of the body. The body is not just those alive, but those who have also died in Christ. Though they have passed, Christ and the Church teach that they still live. Thus, just as we ask for intercession and prayers from members of Christ's body alive today, it is not only acceptable, but advisably we do so with those who have passed, such as from loved

5. For Pope John Paul II, see John Paul II, *Redemptoris*, March 15, 1987. Vatican translation, #24. One finds this citation and the text of John Paul II's reference to Mary as the woman of Revelation 12 at *Wikipedia*, s.v. "Woman of the Apocalypse."

6. For a short article that cogently argues the text has four different referents and not just Mary, see Jimmy Akin's 1997 article entitled "The Woman of Revelation 12."

ones we were/are still close to and especially from the saints. And undoubtedly especially in regards to the most Blessed Virgin Mary. Asking for help via the veneration of saints of the church could have been another section in this concise work but suffice it to say these words succinctly addresses the topic. The successor of Peter, Pope Francis, recently, while citing the *Catechism of the Catholic Church*, 958, three times along with three other sources, wrote the following (see *Amoris Laetitia*, 257, for text and sources):[7]

7. In reading this exhortation, one gets the sense that the text is inspired, which coheres with it coming from the man who now sits in Peter's seat as head of the Church. Among its many purposes, not only is the text a wonderful meditation for clergy and married couples with practical advice, but it could serve as a manual for therapists doing couples counseling, especially for those in the Christian tradition, though not limited to Christians. The present author is one who works with couples in counseling, thus these are not empty words. I recall a similar comment in regards to sensing authority and beauty emanating from above, thus inspired, when reading documents of the Church, specifically differing texts from popes in the book by Scott and Kimberly Hahn, *Rome Sweet Home*. One must read the differing popes and their corresponding documents to really get this sense, an intimation not found in other denominations' documents or books, albeit this is subjective, though nonetheless true for the present author. Perhaps if not willing to read them for yourself, one must take these comments on faith. Regarding Pope Francis and his exhortation, one intuits his emphasis on grace, particularly in the complicated world we live in and in the variety of difficult situations that permeate our culture, such as the rampant divorce rate, blended families, and issues involving disparity of cult. One senses he is more in line with keeping the spirit of the law rather than the letter of the law, something consistent with Jesus. One wonderers if perhaps all people of faith vacillate at times between one of two camps, a legalistic one or a spirt of the law one, not to suggest the law is null and void. It clearly exists for a reason, to help and guide us, but should not be coopted and used as a weapon, and grace, many would argue, supersedes it. Jesus affirmed the law no doubt and told people to sin no more, but one could argue he gave preference to grace. As God, his example is best to follow. His emphasis on God's abiding and ever-present love, grace, and forgiveness is something much needed at this time in our world. That Pope Francis has said the church is a field hospital for the sick resonates with many today who are hurting and is consistent with Jesus' teaching that he came not to call the righteous but sinners (Mark 2:17; Luke 5:32; Matt 9:13). A priest and friend reminded me on Christmas Day 2018 in a private conversation of what was the biggest takeaway of the document for him: that in it the Bishop of Rome explained that God exists in all people, without exception. Indeed, for these reasons it becomes even clearer after reading *Amoris Laetitia* that Pope Francis truly is the successor of Peter,

One way of maintaining fellowship with our loved ones is to pray for them. The Bible tells us that "to pray for the dead" is "holy and pious" (2 *Macc* 12:44–45). "Our prayer for them is capable not only of helping them, but also of making their intercession for us effective." The Book of Revelation portrays the martyrs interceding for those who suffer injustice on earth (cf. *Rev* 6:9–11), in solidarity with this world and its history. Some saints, before dying, consoled their loved ones by promising them that they would be near to help them. Saint Thérèse of Lisieux wished to continue doing good from heaven. Saint Dominic stated the "he would he more helpful after death . . . more powerful in obtaining graces." These are truly "bonds of love," because "the union of the wayfarers with the brethren who sleep in the Lord is in no way interrupted . . . [but] reinforced by an exchange of spiritual goods."

What hope this text brings in understanding that though our loved ones die, they still live, and the love shared between the dead and us still exists. Even the sting of death thus cannot extinguish love! Love transcends death and death is not the end for all of us. We will one day be reunited in love with our loved ones. Hence, a mutually beneficial reciprocity still exists between loved ones, those alive on earth today and those who have already passed on. This again affirms death is not the end and one day we will be reunited with our love ones.

Notice since Protestants are lacking the correct canon of Scripture, they miss out on the 2 Maccabees text in the Hebrew Bible canon. Also, the dead needing our prayers suggests the doctrine of purgatory in this case. Thus, praying to the saints, other Christians who have passed on, members of the body of Christ and notably the blessed Virgin cohere with biblical notions and produce enormous befit.

---

the Bishop of Rome and overseer of the Holy See.

## Marian Apparitions

At the outset it should be stated belief in Marian apparitions, as with Eucharistic miracles and other miracles in the tradition, are not a requirement of the faith.[8] However, these should be investigated, as the Church does, and not outright dismissed. Her apparition in a suburb of Cairo, Zeitoun, where thousands saw her in the late 1960's, including scores of non-Christians, is perhaps the most amazing in my view and can actually be see on YouTube today as well as documentaries. That her apparition was seen by thousands in multiple instances and by many non-Christians is truly amazing! The video is quite astounding; having said that, belief in these apparitions is not a prerequisite for faith or being Catholic. However, one would be hard pressed to try and explain this miracle away. It truly defies any other answer than that the Blessed Virgin appeared.

Our Lady of Fatima with her healing stories as well as the Virgin of Guadalupe who appeared to a peasant boy in modern-day Mexico City in 1531 are also remarkable. That the latter apparition converted a country, the entire population of Mexico, nine million strong, to the faith in a matter of ten years after her appearance where Catholic missionaries, the Franciscans, had ardently tried without success for twenty years prior is a testament to the apparition.[9] Rigorous scientific analysis of the image of our Lady

8. Many do not believe in them, just as many do not believe in all the miracles in the Bible. An Anglican bishop was once quoted as saying, "He who believes in all the miracles in the Bible is an idiot. He who believes in none of them is an even bigger idiot." This is wise counsel, and time constraints preclude delving into this topic further. There is really one miracle, however, I would argue is required to be believed in if one considers themselves a Christian: the resurrection of Christ. As Paul said in 1 Cor 15:17, "If Christ has not been raised, your faith is futile and you are still in your sins." To be Catholic, I would argue it is also requisite the real presence of Christ in the Eucharist be believed.

9. This was originally brought to my attention by the remarkable ministry of Bishop Robert Barron and his Word on Fire Ministries. This was discussed in one of the ministries of his daily emails sent that reflects on the daily gospel reading. I received it during Advent on Wednesday, December 12, 2018, on the Feast of Our Lady of Guadalupe.

of Guadalupe on the tilma of Juan Diego has been undergone. Juan Diego was instructed by the apparition to bring flowers to the archbishop at the time, and after doing so and opening up the tilma, the flowers fell to the floor and the miraculous image of Our Lady of Guadalupe appeared on the tilma. The image is now housed in the Basilica of Our Lady of Guadalupe in Mexico City. Tests confirm the image was not painted and fascinatingly when looked at through a microscope her eyes show an image of Juan Diego; the image miraculously remains at the normal temperature of a human, 98.6 degrees. It is remarkable how the image has not decayed by now considering how old it is. This calls to mind how many of the bodies of the saints also do not seem to decay. These are known as the incorruptible saints, and lists along with images of them can be found online. God seems to preserve them in a very special way, perhaps so the faithful can come see them and be strengthened in their faith.

There are indeed countless stories of Mary's intercession bringing healings, such as the story of her helping a German couple heal their marriage in the seventeenth century. Father Jakob Rem is said to have held up their marriage ribbon, a custom of the time symbolizing their union, to an image of "Our Lady of the Snows" and the ribbon miraculously turned bright white. Following this miracle, the marriage was mended. This became the basis for the now popular and growing devotion Pope Francis brought back to South America after studying for his doctorate in Germany, the devotion of Our Lady Undoer of Knots. This is a favorite of Pope Francis today. There are countless other miracle stories associated with Marian apparitions in which she often performs a miracle, and it is to be noted she always points to her son, Jesus the Christ.

## Rosary

Thus, it has been seen how very biblical the prayer of the Rosary is, not to mention the countless people who have found it enormously powerful. It was seen how most of the Rosary originally given to St. Dominic in a vision of the blessed Virgin in 1214 CE is very biblical. On a personal note, not only has the Rosary given countless people throughout the ages comfort, help, and a deeper connection to God, it has for the present author. No wonder Pope John Paul II stressed its importance so much in his pontificate. True *ahavah* (love) and *shalom* (peace) flow from its practice. Though this method of prayer is a later development of the Church, its helpful tradition has endorsed it repeatedly to the benefit of millions. Yet again, tradition is shown to be important here.

To recap, let us again notice some of the amazing verses from Scripture when the angel Gabriel visits Mary. Luke 1:28 reads, "And he came to her and said, 'Greetings, favored one! The Lord is with you.'" This can be translated Hail Mary full of Grace (*hesed* in Hebrew), the Lord is with you! A few verses later in Luke 1:42, upon seeing Mary, her cousin Elizabeth, who is pregnant with John the Baptist, who leaps in his womb toward Jesus (v. 41), exclaims, "with a loud cry, 'Blessed are you among women, and blessed is the fruit of your womb.'" Luke 1:48b then has Mary prophetically explain, "From now on all generations will call me blessed." That this is all biblical is likely surprising to many Protestants, and that such praise is heaped upon her. This makes perfect sense seeing God choose her to bear the Son of God. Again, one need remember that in the prayer of the Rosary, Mary is petitioned to pray for us, not worshipped in her own right. She is implored for our intercession before God and she always points to God, bringing people to her son Jesus.

I know many stories of individuals who ardently pray the Rosary daily and find healing or help for themselves or those they incorporate into the prayer and ask for help in the prayer. Mediation of the holy ministries of the Rosary also brings one closer to God, and contemplative prayer can and often does follow. Following the brilliance of St. Ignatius of Loyola and his classic *The Spiritual Exercises*, it has been suggested that one simply pray the Rosary one time very slowly, pondering each word in depth, meditating on each word.[10] The present author did this to much benefit and

---

10. This brilliant idea arising out of the work of St. Ignatius suggesting another way to pray, praying slowly well-known prayers and pondering them

insight. It is commended to all. Mary is the gateway for many that brings them to Christ. That is precisely what she desires to do, and what she has told individuals in her apparitions. They demonstrate this point. A friend once told me you can be close to Christ but you are even closer to him if you are close to his mother.

---

in-depth, can be found in *The Spiritual Exercises*, and was brought to my attention in Father Ed Broom's article "Saint Gertrude and the Golden Hail Mary."

Chapter VI

# The Sacraments, Specifically the Sacrament of Reconciliation

A SACRAMENT HAS TRADITIONALLY been defined as an outward expression or visible sign of an inward grace. Catholics and Protestants agree on this, thought they do not on the number of sacraments. Catholics understand seven and Protestants understand only two. All seven sacraments are instituted by God, not just the two of Protestants. The seven sacraments are: Baptism, Confirmation, Reconciliation/Penance, Holy Orders, Matrimony, Anointing the Sick, and the Eucharist.[1] Interestingly seven is a number that symbolizes wholeness or completeness to the ancients, especially the ancient Hebrews, so the seven days of creation in Genesis. The Church therefore has the whole or completeness in their sacramental system. Protestants do agree that baptism and communion are sacraments,[2] which is interest-

1. Time constraints preclude delving into each of the seven sacrament in this short work. Suffice it to say the reader can find an abundance of information on each of the sacraments by consulting the *Catechism of the Catholic Church* or *The Compendium: Catechism of the Catholic Church*, books on each sacrament or apologetic books for the faith, and even on the internet on helpful websites such as Catholic Answers or Catholics Come Home. These resources will provide the biblical texts that show where Jesus instituted each sacrament. For where each sacrament can be found in the Bible as well as the catechism, one can see: http://www.agapebiblestudy.com/charts/The%20Seven%20Sacraments%20Instituted%20by%20Jesus%20Christ.htm.

2. It needs to be noted that from a Catholic perspective communion among Protestants is not the same as the Eucharist, and Catholics do not understand

ing considering some Protestant theology affirms only accepting Christ is necessary for salvation. However, they would likely argue when one accepts Christ you are being baptized at the moment by the Holy Spirit, although that is not the case with most Protestant denominations, especially mainline Protestantism.[3]

Sacrament means something that is holy, thus by nature a mystery to some degree to us. The important thing for us is that God instituted them and this can be seen on the pages in Scripture. It records the institution of the sacraments by God. So, for example, the sacrament of marriage—who can honestly say that in the depth

---

the "real presence" of Christ in the bread and wine when communion is offered at their services. Pastors are not ordained priests and thus do not actually administer the sacrament. Catholics are advised not to partake in communion of Protestant services. Though some priests suggest Christ would never turn anyone away from him, and specifically from him in the Eucharist, the official stance of the Church is that non-Catholics should not partake in the Eucharist. On this issue, one should recall the words of St. Paul in 1 Cor 11:27: "Whoever, therefore, eats the bread or drinks the cup of the Lord in an unworthy manner will be answerable for the body and blood of the Lord." This again does point to the real presence in the Eucharist.

3. The well-known mainline Protestant denominations include Anglicans, Lutherans, Presbyterians, and Methodists. In recent years, their numbers have been declining rapidly and they have tended to splinter apart and continue to do so. Independent evangelical churches have grown in number for years but have seen a decline in the last couple of years. This is likely part of a larger trend in the West, particularly in America, of a more secular culture. America seems to be going the way of Europe in becoming more secular. That is why it is argued the mission field today is no longer third-word countries such as in South America, but rather, first-world countries such as those in Europe. It is ironic that these are the countries that have a more educated population and the countries where Christianity first took hold. Perhaps as education increases, so does ego and people think they know better that God, thus becoming their own God. Education in and of itself is not bad. It is an individualism that each person thinks they know best and what constitutes right and wrong that is troublesome, as well as a failure to submit to authority and at least listen to the wisdom and arguments the Church makes. That a moral relativism pervades our secular society is also troublesome and that is precisely why Pope John Paul II strenuously fought against such an idea, almost prophetically so, as he could see what it would bring and is bringing. One often forgets it is the church that built Western civilization. The Catholic Church invented universities, science, hospitals, and preserved the classics of literature. On this see Woods, *How the Catholic Church Built Western Civilization*.

of their soul they do not already know it to be a holy mystery and sacrament? It reflects God's love for his church, thus the love God has for us is reflected and experientially revealed and learned in marriage. Thus, it is a sacrament and blessing from God.[4]

The sacrament of baptism is a very important one, for it brings one into the church, as opposed to the must accept Jesus and be born again theology in some Protestant circles. This reductionist theology will be discussed in the next section. Baptism washes away origin sin that Adam incurred for humanity.[5] The "born again" biblical text in John is actually a reference to baptism. Protestants miss this point and usually quote the text and leave out the ending that references baptism in its referencing water, thus getting the text wrong and taking it out of context. This has led to an incorrect, nonbiblical theology that would have been foreign to Jesus: namely, that one does not become a Christian and get saved until they accept Jesus in their hearts.[6] Not only does this contradict the entirety of Scripture and Jesus' teaching, but it ignores the sacraments of baptism and reconciliation, both instituted by Jesus

---

4. This is not to deny our sinful nature can corrupt a marriage and make it go horrible awry. It has rightly been said by many that any marriage needs three people in it to truly work, both partners and Jesus. Interestingly, it is the number three, the same number as the Holy Trinity. Though the term *trinity* is not mentioned in Scripture, it clearly is present. One need only see the Great Commission (Matt 28:16–20), which all scholars concur is original and not a later addition to the gospel, as such does exist (so, e.g., Jesus crying blood in the Garden of Gethsemane in Luke's Gospel; it does not appear in our earliest manuscripts).

5. Granted the doctrine of original sin does not get called this or fully articulated until St. Augustine in the fourth century CE; however, that is not to deny it is not true and biblical. It just does not get fully articulated until later, as with so many of our doctrines, but this reveals the importance of later church tradition for articulating the faith. This is why hundreds of years later the English Anglican convert to Catholicism Cardinal John Henry Newman so uplifted the importance of doctrine, a term many today regrettably do not like.

6. Some have told me that after they prayed the "salvation prayer" of accepting Jesus into their heart they later would frequently do it repeatedly out of fear it did not take the first time. Catholic theology is very different and one does not hear these type of stories among Catholics. This specific fear does not seem to exist for obvious reasons.

himself for the church to engage in up until his coming again or Second Coming. This will be further addressed below in the section on "Not by Faith Alone." In its entirety the baptism text sorely misread by many Protestants reads:

> Now there was a Pharisee named Nicodemus, a leader of the Jews. He came to Jesus by night and said to him, "Rabbi, we know that you are a teacher who has come from God; for no one can do these signs that you do apart from the presence of God." Jesus answered him, "Very truly, I tell you, no one can see the kingdom of God without being born from above." Nicodemus said to him, "How can anyone be born after having grown old? Can one enter a second time into the mother's womb and be born?" Jesus answered, "Very truly, I tell you, no one can enter the kingdom of God without being born of water and Spirit. What is born of the flesh is flesh, and what is born of the Spirit is spirit. Do not be astonished that I said to you, 'You must be born from above.' The wind blows where it chooses, and you hear the sound of it, but you do not know where it comes from or where it goes. So it is with everyone who is born of the Spirit." Nicodemus said to him, "How can these things be?" Jesus answered him, "Are you a teacher of Israel, and yet you do not understand these things? Very truly, I tell you, we speak of what we know and testify to what we have seen; yet you do not receive our testimony. If I have told you about earthly things and you do not believe, how can you believe if I tell you about heavenly things? No one has ascended into heaven except the one who descended from heaven, the Son of Man. And just as Moses lifted up the serpent in the wilderness, so must the Son of Man be lifted up, that whoever believes in him may have eternal life. For God so loved the world that he gave his only Son, so that everyone who believes in him may not perish but may have eternal life. Indeed, God did not send the Son into the world to condemn the world, but in order that the world might be saved through him. Those who believe in him are not condemned; but those who do not believe are condemned already, because they have not believed in the name of the only Son of God. And this

is the judgment, that the light has come into the world, and people loved darkness rather than light because their deeds were evil. For all who do evil hate the light and do not come to the light, so that their deeds may not be exposed. But those who do what is true come to the light, so that it may be clearly seen that their deeds have been done in God." After this Jesus and his disciples went into the Judean countryside, and he spent some time there with them and baptized. John also was baptizing at Aenon near Salim because water was abundant there; and people kept coming and were being baptized—John, of course, had not yet been thrown into prison. Now a discussion about purification arose between John's disciples and a Jew. They came to John and said to him, "Rabbi, the one who was with you across the Jordan, to whom you testified, here he is baptizing, and all are going to him." John answered, "No one can receive anything except what has been given from heaven." (John 3:1–27)

It is true that the New Testament is rather explicit on two requisite, nonnegotiable elements of the faith one must do: be baptized (see 1 Cor 12:13; Acts 22:16, which explains it washes away sins) and confess Jesus is Lord and believe in his resurrection and one will be saved (for the latter two see Rom 10:9). Mark 16:16 reads, "The one who believes and is baptized will be saved; but the one who does not believe will be condemned." It is interesting to note that baptism is not a choice in the Bible but rather a commandment. And notice what the first Bishop of Rome writes: 1 Peter 3:21 reads, "And baptism, which this prefigured, now saves you—not as a removal of dirt from the body, but as an appeal to God for a good conscience, through the resurrection of Jesus Christ."

Thus, the sacrament of baptism is essential. Baptism washes away original sin, then penance or the sacrament of reconciliation is needed for all sin that occurs after the regenerative water of baptism. Reconciliation, in which a Catholic goes to confession to confess his sins to a priest, and then is given absolution by the priest and penance to do, cleanses the soul of both venial and mortal sins, both of which have consequences, only the latter having an eternal, grave consequence if not forgiven in this life by

God.[7] Reconciliation ensures without any doubt for the participant that forgiveness is mediated to the supplicant because of the priest's role as acting in the person of Christ (*in persona Christi*). The priest helps to facilitate and mediate forgiveness from God. What a blessing given by God that brings peace and assurance, something so many are lacking because of past sins. People often cannot forgiven themselves and beat themselves up their entire life because they have not been brought into the faith and received this blessing from God of knowledge that one is truly forgiven.[8] I have

7. Venial sins hurt a person's soul and their relationship to God. Reconciliation and also the beautiful doctrine of purgatory addressed already take care of these sins. Mortal sins lead to damnation if not forgiven by God, which the wonderful sacrament of reconciliation offers—namely forgiveness by God of both mortal and venial sins. For a sin to be mortal, three conditions must be met: (1) Its subject matter must be grave. (2) It must be committed with full knowledge (and awareness) of the sinful action and the gravity of the offense. (3) It must be committed with deliberate and complete consent. The Church does not have a specific list of mortal sins. Breaking the Ten Commandments are usually consider mortal sins, along with adultery, fornication and blasphemy, among others. On mortal sins, one should consult "IV. The Gravity of Sin: Mortal and Venial Sin," CCC 1854–1864; here one will find what constitutes "grave," among other helpful information on the important subject.

8. No doubt, receiving absolution and knowing one's sins are forgiven can have a profound psychological impact. Just carrying around sins can have an impact on one's psyche and well-being, even if one has not sinned and thinks they have. A case in point: I taught an Introduction to Religion class at a university, in which I had a veteran. We were discussing morality in the different religious traditions in the class and I happened to be discussing the Ten Commandments, as we were discussing the Abrahamic faith traditions that day. I made the off comment that a proper translation of the commandment regrading taking life is "thou shall not kill" not "thou shall not murder." I explained the difference between the terms and how killing is permissible and society allows it in certain situations. The veteran came up to me after class completely relieved. He had been walking around for some years feeling he had sinned by what he had done in the line of duty. I explained he had not broken the commandment of not murdering, that killing is permissible in self-defense and in other instances in the military. The relief from knowing he was no longer carrying around what he thought was a sin was visible on his face and even palpable. This demonstrated the tremendous psychological impact carrying sins around can have, as in this case a young man was being impacting in a large manner and he had not even sinned. He only thought he had. Hence, reconciliation is vital so one can truly know they are forgiven via the

actually had a person tell me they had pure euphoria after receiving absolution from the priest and praying the act of contrition. If only all of humanity could experience such! What a different world it would be.[9]

A common Protestant objection is that confessing your sins to a priest instead of going straight to God in some way cheapens the sacrifice of Christ. At first glance, this seems like there might be a good point here. However, the biblical evidence suggests we do make use of the sacrament and the church teaches we do too unless otherwise not able to do so. In fact, Catholics can in some instances go straight to God, but it is advisable for several reasons to partake of the sacrament. Regarding the Protestant objection, it is not the case it cheapens the sacrifice of Christ and one must understand the forgiveness received in the sacrament Jesus instituted is still given and comes because of one sacrifice of Christ on the cross. Additionally, because of church tradition, as has been shown to be important, the sacrament gets fleshed out later in history in regards the details of how it tangibly occurs in the church, as the specifics were not explicitly provided by Jesus. Not only is this permissible, but also expected of the church as God's representatives on earth. Christ works through his people to figure out the details and expects such, and expects in some instances to adapt things for the times the church finds itself in, which is the context the church finds itself without compromising the faith and its doctrines. This betrays the importance of tradition yet again, tradition in maintaining the faith but being able to adapt it to some extent as needed provided the essentials of what is vital and passed on remain.[10] The pragmatics of how reconciliation tangibly occurs has

---

mediation of the forgiveness of sins by a priest through the means instituted by Christ recorded in the Bible.

9. To be sure, the sacrament has evolved over the centuries and did not exist in the early church in the form it now takes. However, the form it takes is biblical and the magisterium of the church ensures it is consistent and done in a manner God desires, as it holds the keys to bind and loose and possesses the authority of implementing sacraments and making decisions on important matters of faith, such as how this sacrament is done today.

10. That the church must always find new ways to translate and proclaim

changed slightly over the ages and might in the future, provided the fundamentals stay the same. Christ expects his representatives, as caretakers of his flock, to address and handle these types of matters here on earth until he comes again.

Regarding the biblical mandates, the Bible says to confess our sins to one another. James 5:16 reads, "Therefore confess your sins to one another, and pray for one another, so that you may be healed. The prayer of the righteous is powerful and effective." The sacrament of reconciliation fulfills this mandate. That the disciples are given the power to forgive and retains sins (cf. John 20:21–23) will be addressed below presently and apostolic succession implies their successors are given the power to carry on the process until Christ's Second Coming. The sacrament of reconciliation is a very beautiful sacrament many Catholics do not partake in enough. Can we not just go to Christ directly as Protestants desire?—Sure but the sacrament makes it better and is required, for it fulfills James 5:16 above. Christ likely knew the psychological dimension of the priest acting in the person of Christ and mediating absolution has on a person. I have heard stories of tremendous relief that comes that likely does not when simply confessing to God with a contrite heart on one's own. There is also a doubt that one is truly forgiven and people tend to confess the sin repeatedly when this is done outside of the help of the sacrament.

The sacrament cleanses the soul of both mortal and venial sins. Sometimes Protestants object to such a distinction, arguing sin is sin and there is no distinction. First, that is not the case. Some sins are worse than others, as the Bible makes clear. Logically, we all inherently know this to be true, as it is written on our hearts, our conscious (cf. Rom 2:15). If looking for a distinction in regards to sin in the Bible, one need only recall 1 John 5:17: "All wrongdoing is sin, but there is sin that is not mortal." Elsewhere it is clear that there are mortal sins of grave, eternal consequences

---

the gospel message for differing cultures and contexts is also presupposed here. It is the same message always, but often the vocabulary must be changed and updated for modern times and different cultures, much as explaining the real presence in the Eucharist likely needs to be updated for our modern times.

(cf. Gal 5:19–21; Rom 1:28–32, among many other texts) So, there is a hierarchy of sins, or more specially a differentiation between mortal and venial sins clearly laid out in the Bible. The sacrament of reconciliation is absolutely necessary to address our mortal sins as well as venial, both of which occur after original sin is wiped out with baptism and all other sin if one is baptized later in life. The sacrament addresses the sins committed after baptism through the one and final sacrifice of Christ. Although if one passes with a mortal sin on them, one is in danger of eternal separation from God, it needs to be remembered venial sins are forgiven but penance must still be paid and likely for most this will occur in purgatory as addressed already.

To summarize, as noted sometimes Protestants object to going before a priest to confess sins, and rather argue one only need go straight to God. It needs to be recalled James says to confess sins to one another and the church has been given the keys to forgive and retains sins. These mandates are completed in the sacrament. Regarding the disciples, and we know the subsequent church, being given the power to forgive sins, one need read the following:

> Jesus said to them again, "Peace be with you. As the Father has sent me, so I send you." When he had said this, he breathed on them and said to them, "Receive the Holy Spirit. If you forgive the sins of any, they are forgiven them; if you retain the sins of any, they are retained." (John 20:21–23)

Going to the sacrament instituted by Jesus, as opposed to confessing directly to him, in no way cheapens the sacrifice of Christ, for through the sacrament of reconciliation the priest is mediating forgiveness through the already one and final sacrifice of Christ for the entire world (1 John 2:2). Furthermore, again, there are indeed provisions in the *Catechism* for going straight to God when going to the sacrament is not possible, provided a contrite heart is present.

Due to the doctrine of apostolic succession and the bishops ordaining priests to carry on the work of the church, and because Christ instituted the sacrament of reconciliation as seen in John, it is clear the priest acting in the person of Christ has the power to mediate God's forgiveness/absolution because of the atoning work of Christ. It has been seen how this sacrament also provides for the mandate in James to confess sins to another. Regarding the disciples being given such power from Christ that is passed on in the church, one need cite John 20:22–23 again: "When he had said this, he breathed on them and said to them, 'Receive the Holy Spirit. If you forgive the sins of any, they are forgiven them; if you retain the sins of any, they are retained.'" One cannot argue with this. Jesus clearly gave his later followers this incredible power.

# Chapter VII

# Not by Faith Alone

MOST PROTESTANTS, ESPECIALLY OUR evangelical brothers and sisters, adhere to the belief one is: saved by faith alone. The Bible actually explicitly says the exact opposite! James 2:24 reads: "You see that a person is justified by works and *not by faith alone*."[1] It is curious in light of this text that the notion of faith alone has been the salient staple and tenant or rallying cry for the Reformation and for Protestantism. No wonder Martin Luther wanted James thrown out of the Bible. Providence would not have it, and thank goodness considering the blessing the book is, particularly its emphasis on perseverance through trial in the beginning of the letter.[2]

Thus, Martin Luther's most fundamental rallying cry is also stated this way: Justification by faith alone.[3] It was Luther's core

1. One should consult the monumental treatment by Sungenis, *Not by Faith Alone*, as well as VanLandingham, *Judgement & Justification in Early Judaism and the Apostle Paul*. Horn, *Case for Catholicism*, also has two helpful chapters devoted to the subject (10 & 11 entitled "Justification, Part I" and "Justification, Part II," 201–37).

2. These verses come to mind: Jas 1:2–4: "My brothers and sisters, whenever you face trials of any kind, consider it nothing but joy, because you know that the testing of your faith produces endurance; and let endurance have its full effect, so that you may be mature and complete, lacking in nothing." And Jas 1:12: "Blessed is anyone who endures temptation. Such a one has stood the test and will receive the crown of life that the Lord has promised to those who love him."

3. One can see how this might be an alluring theology for some, as it is rather simple and does not require much thinking or holding oneself accountable. So, to be sure, the theology is convenient in its simplicity but too

doctrine and one could argue the core doctrine of the Reformation. Justification essentially means to make one right before God; thus, it means if one is justified in theological parlance one is saved from damnation and receives entry into heaven and eternal life. Faith here refers to faith in Jesus Christ, that is a belief in his divinity and atoning work on the cross. As important as both are, they do not paint the full picture. Ironically, not only does the testimony of Jesus and Scripture not cohere with justification by faith alone, but also it is nowhere to be found in the writings of the church fathers! It is not even to be found in St. Augustine, a particular favorite of Protestants. Interestingly, second-generation reformers such as Calvin seem to uplift more of a sacramental theology at times, arguing strenuously for baptism often. This misdirected, or incorrect notion of Luther would lead much later to the view that one need only be born again to be saved, which it has been seen is a misreading of John's Gospel in chapter 3, which references baptism in regards to being born anew, again or from above.

This "born again" theology of being saved at the point one accepts Jesus and then one truly becomes a Christian is a late development. It begins with James Whitfield in the eighteenth century. He taught it is not until one is born again and saved that one is considered to become truly a saved Christian,[4] an idea completely

---

reductionist and wrong, ultimately. Unfortunately, it is misleading and simply wrong when tested against the Bible, ironically the only supposed source for many Protestants according to *sola Scriptura*.

4. Whitfield's notion coheres with another Protestant notion that is too a surprisingly late development: that Scripture is to be read and taken literally (e.g., reading Genesis 1 and 2 as literal or viewing Jonah as literally in the belly of some sort of fish for three days). It is clear from the early church fathers up into the present that the Catholic Church has always understood that not all of the Bible it to be taken literally. Recall reading Genesis literally is one reason it took so long for St. Augustine to convert to the faith; he did so after learning from St. Ambrose, Bishop of Milan, that texts could be inspired and from God but do not have to be read literally. Early church fathers or patristic writings reveal the creation accounts in Genesis were not read literally by the early church, as such is a late development that had its beginnings in England. The Protestant Reformation helped pave the way for it with its emphasis on the plain meaning of a text. Now, it is a different discussion altogether when discussing the New Testament, as I would argue it should be read in a more

not attested in Scripture; it is simply not biblical and not taught by Christ, or seen in the writings of those immediately following Christ in the early church or even in later church documents. Recall, he instituted the sacramental system, especially baptism and reconciliation for salvation. This is not to deny the Eucharist does not play a role along with needing to forgive people (Matt 6:15; 18:35)[5] and other good works (Jas 2:24) in regards to our eternal salvation. Common logic and our intuition/conscience alone tells us one cannot be a mass murder and these actions or works do not have a bearing on one's soul.

That a prayer (e.g., the Salvation Prayer) and intellectual assent to Christ gets one saved and at that moment one becomes a Christian is not only a late development and not biblical, but it is wrong and irresponsible. It does not take into account the sacramental system instituted by Christ or the Bible's testimony on works. Again, the notion one is saved and justified by faith alone and it does not matter what one does, so someone can go commit mass murder and still be saved, is not only ridiculous but

---

literal sense, as history writing does exist at this time. When the Hebrew Bible was written, it did not exist. It does not enter the world stage until Herodotus in the Hellenistic era as noted earlier, so is it alright to anachronistically apply our modern stands back onto ancient writers who did not have the same standards for writing history like we do, such as being free to embellish, which today is not acceptable? I think not; thus, the church is correct in not reading as literal all of Scripture as in a historical sense such as the creation accounts in Gen 1 and 2. However, it is more appropriate to read the New Testament in a more literal fashion and as containing what we today call history, for the genre does exist by the time Christ enters history. Also, recall the gospels seem to be their own kind of genre. The medieval historian from Oxford C. S. Lewis said that he knew ancient myths and the gospels do not have the feel of myth. That they were written in Koine Greek also suggests they were intended for widespread dissemination, not to mention they are not written in elevated prose like the ancient myths were. They seem to be intended for the everyday common person and seem to be a historical biography that likely can and should be read more literally than the Hebrew Bible, as history writing by this time does in fact exist. The gospels seem to be a type of hybrid of theological biography with history and perhaps some myth. One should recall myth does not equate with not true; myths can reveal profound truths.

5. In these biblical texts, Jesus in his ministry specifically explains that it is imperative for our eternal well-being that we forgive one another.

irresponsible.[6] After Whitfield, this erroneous idea influenced D. L. Moody among others, including the late and exceedingly moral, well-meaning, and influential Billy Graham. It influences much of Protestant evangelical society today and has a firm foothold in America. Unfortunately, it is factually wrong and ironically not biblical. Usually those espousing it also espouse a *sola Scriptura* view and do not even realize their soteriology is not only not biblical but rather a highly selective reading of texts, which uses a few proof texts and throws out the rest of Scripture and essentially all of church history since the time of Christ, not to mention the testimony of Jesus.

A few verses earlier, before his famous line that a person is justified by works and *not by faith alone*, in his letter, James explains, "What good is it, my brothers and sisters, if you say you have faith but do not have works? Can faith save you?" (2:14) He also writes, "But someone will say, 'You have faith and I have works.' Show me your faith apart from your works, and I by my works will show you my faith" (2:18). It is actually rather remarkable that in v. 22 of the same chapter he writes regrading the patriarch Abraham in Genesis: "You see that faith was active along with his works, and faith was brought to completion by the works." In demonstrating the mutual reciprocity of both faith and works, James eloquently continues and reads, "For just as the body without the spirit is dead, so faith without works is also dead" (Jas 2:26).

Without question, then, both are of vital importance. As noted already above, one need recall that the text from John of being born again is often misinterpreted and not read in context as referring to baptism, but rather, erroneously as accepting Christ and being saved once and for all, thus it follows what one does has no bearing on one's next life. James explains this is not

---

6. I have heard on more than one occasion individuals being introduced to the notion of being saved and then it does not matter what one does as shocking to people at first. It is as though in our core we inherently know there is something wrong with this view, which again is not biblical or Catholic. The "once saved always saved" view that some Calvinists espouse is not biblical in the least. Recall Phil 2:12b reads, ". . .work out your own salvation with fear and trembling."

the case as suggested in these texts above, along with the entirety of Scripture and the teaching magisterium of the church established by Christ whose tradition is safeguarded and passed on via apostolic succession, the unbroken chain that goes all the way back to the disciples and Christ himself.

To be sure, both Catholics and Protestants share much in common. Often our biggest quarrels are with those we share the most in common. Life has taught us all this is often the case. Martin Luther is a prime example in regards to Christian relations with the Jews, as he originally had good relationships with the local Jewish population, but they became strained and a robust animosity arose for him when he could not convert them. His later writings about the Jewish people are a travesty and so is the fact that later under National Socialism in Germany Adolph Hitler often quoted Luther. So, for example both traditions affirm similar things, such as both agree Christ's sacrifice saves, and was a one-time act, and we are saved by grace through faith and it is a completely unmerited gift from God, not of our works (Eph 2:8–9). This is true of our baptism and salvation in Christ.[7] Recall what the people in the Acts of the Apostles ask Peter and the disciples; notice here Peter once again stands out:

> Now when they heard this, they were cut to the heart and said to Peter and to the other apostles, "Brothers, what should we do?" Peter said to them, "*Repent, and be baptized every one of you in the name of Jesus Christ so that your sins may be forgiven; and you will receive the gift of the Holy Spirit.* For the promise is for you, for your children, and for all who are far away, everyone whom the Lord our God calls to him." (Acts 2:37–39)

Catholicism correctly teaches that sins after baptism need to be addressed and they are through the same sacrifice of Christ mediated to us through the sacrament of reconciliation. But one must not discount one's behavior or sins and realize our sins have a bearing on our eternal destiny. The book of James makes this very clear. The Bible and patristic works or the church fathers

---

7. Horn, *Case for Catholicism*, 199–200.

both concur that the possibility of losing one's salvation exists, as opposed to certain Reformed branches of Calvinism, hence the need for the sacrament of reconciliation. Common logic and our intuition, conscience or the spirt in us also confirms this in our hearts if we are truly honest with ourselves. Furthermore, recall the important topic of forgiveness noted above—Jesus in his ministry explains it is imperative for our eternal well-being that we forgive one another (Matt 6:15; 18:35).[8] Matthew 6:15 reads, "But if you do not forgive others, neither will your Father forgive your trespasses." This is an action tied in to our salvation consistent with comments in the book of St. James and the totality of Jesus' ministry, as well as Paul's. It is clearly not consistent with justification by faith alone! It is therefore not consistent with Protestantism and this comes from the Bible!

Particularly regarding Pauline literature, some have argued there is a tension in his writings; however, upon close examination, there is not. New understandings of Paul have arisen in scholarship, usually referred to as the New Perspective on Paul,[9] clarifying

8. That forgiveness is vital in life cannot be overstated. There are stories of people having miraculous healings from major diseases such as cancer purely by enacting the hard work of forgiving everyone in their lives that need being forgiven. Forgiveness is more for the one forgiving than the one being forgiven. Psychology has demonstrated the active ingredient for true forgiveness is empathy, an empathy for the other needing to be forgiven and their plight in life. Research suggests that is the key as well as that it needs to be seen as a process. Interestingly, there are meditation techniques that can help with it. For some, see the present author's *Manifesting Peace*. Unforgiveness wreaks havoc on a person's soul and body. Additionally, not only is it needed on an individual level but on a corporate, group, and global level. One could argue a lack of forgives played a role in WWII. The allies were mad and perhaps over-punished Germany after WWI in the treaty of Versailles. Consequently, Germany was angry, humiliated, and embarrassed about the treaty and how it left them, as a country and individually; thus, twenty years after WWI the world was at war again. Had the allies or Germany individually and collectively worked on or demonstrated more forgiveness, perhaps things would have been different. Thus, forgiveness is vital not only for individuals and one's well-being, but for groups as well, such as nation states. Wars could be averted if only forgiveness could be granted, not to mention countless lawsuits and all the differing problems that arise in society and for individuals when it is not present.

9. One should see Sanders, *Paul and Palestinian Judaism*; Dunn, *New*

his letters, theology, and understanding of the law. The movement affirms his Jewish background and shows he was not opposed to the torah or law per se, as has commonly been thought.[10] It has been discovered that

> the problem for Paul was not people who chose works over grace in order to become right with God. The problem was people who chose grace given to a chosen people who obeyed the Torah (or Jews) over grace being given to all people who have faith in Christ and subsequently obey "the law of Christ" (Gal 6:2; 1 Cor 9:21).[11]

This is but one of the more salient aspects of many arising out of a new, more correct understanding of Paul, one applicable for the topic at hand. With its beginning in the late 1970s, the New Perspective on Paul, which corrected erroneous views of Judaism in the time of Jesus and Paul's teaching on justification, "showed how many Protestants anachronistically read sixteenth-century debates between the Reformers and the Catholic Church back into Paul's arguments."[12] On the important subject of Paul's view of the law, T. Horn helpfully cites the well-known New Testament scholar Bart Ehrman:

> When Paul speaks of "works" he is explicitly referring to "works of the law," that is, observance of Jewish rules governing circumcision, the Sabbath, kosher foods and the like. When James speaks of works, he means something

---

*Perspective on Paul.* The work of N. T. Wight is also very helpful.

10. After all, recall the words of Jesus in his affirming of the law, which would have been consistent with Paul in his day: Matt 5:17–19: "Do not think that I have come to abolish the law or the prophets; I have come not to abolish but to fulfill. For truly I tell you, until heaven and earth pass away, not one letter, not one stroke of a letter, will pass from the law until all is accomplished. Therefore, whoever breaks one of the least of these commandments, and teaches others to do the same, will be called least in the kingdom of heaven; but whoever does them and teaches them will be called great in the kingdom of heaven."

11. Horn, *Case for Catholicism*, 223.

12. Horn, *Case for Catholicism*, 220.

like "good deeds." Paul himself would not argue that a person could have faith without doing good deeds.[13]

Thus, when the Apostle Paul is speaking of "works," it is in regards to following laws that set one apart as Jewish, not good deeds and works in general. Context is thus key for understanding Paul. One need recall Paul's self-identity throughout his life was one in which he remains a Jew; even after his conversion he explicitly states he is one (Act 22:3). He does not break with Judaism but rather views Jesus fulfilling it. Horn explains:

> Paul's complaint wasn't that his fellow Jews were trying to earn their standing before God through good works. Rather, his complaint was that they preached the need to become a Jew (or enter into God's Old Covenant) before one could become a Christian and enter into God's New Covenant.[14]

This issue eventually culminated in the Jerusalem Council in 48 CE with the resolution that Gentiles need not first become Jews or observe Mosaic laws to become Christian. Such was not requisite for Christians. Undoubtedly, this is an exceedingly complicated topic, but suffice it to say there is no tension or ambiguity regarding the issue of grace and works in Paul, particularly, and the biblical text in general. Time constraints preclude delving into this topic further. The reader is recommend to study T. Horn's chapter "Justification, Part II," in *A Case for Catholicism*, for a concise, helpful analysis. Suffice it to say, Horn eloquently concludes his chapter "Justification, Part II" with a most helpful quote regarding salvation in the Catholic understanding:

> The only thing they "must do" in order to be saved is not remain in a state of unrepentant, mortal sin until the end of their lives. Quoting *Lumen Gentium*, the *Catechisms* says, "All men may attain salvation through faith,

---

13. Horn, *Case for Catholicism*, 223. For the citation, see Ehrman, *Peter, Paul and Mary Magdalene*, 167.

14. Horn, *Case for Catholicism*, 222.

Baptism and the observance of the Commandments"
(*LG* 24; (*CCC* 2068).[15]

Could the *Catechism of the Catholic Church* Horn cites here
be any clearer or more concise on salvation from a Catholic perspective? What a treasure trove of information/teaching the *Catechism* offers, even in this one line. We fool ourselves if we think
what we do, such as not following the commandments, such as
the Ten Commandments, does not matter.[16] The *Catechism* clearly
states here it does, and recall it comes from the magisterium of
the church instituted by Christ to guide us. Thus, the *Catechism*
represents tradition safeguarded and passed on for our benefit.
Logically, we know that what we do and the observance of the
commandments matters and the teaching on this score in the
Bible and *Catechism* are true, not to mention God has written it in
our hearts (Rom 2:15).

Therefore, enough of the Protestant view if we only believe in
Christ we are saved and it does not matter what we do, even if we
cheat on our wives or commit murder. The totality of Scripture,
the teachings of Jesus' as well as Paul, the early church and magisterium of the church throughout history and up until today, safeguarded and passed on because of apostolic succession[17] concurs

---

15. Horn, *Case for Catholicism*, 237.

16. An oft-overlooked story in regards to the importance of following the
commandments is the story of the woman caught in adultery that Jesus saves
from being stoned to death found in John 8:1–11. Though she had, in fact,
sinned by breaking one of the Ten Commandments, as she was caught in adultery, Jesus did not condemn her. However, he did say "go and sin no more" (v.
11). This shows God was gracious but at the same time expected/required her
to stop her sinning and obey the torah. What she did or that works matter is
without question here; Jesus wanted her to obey the law, thus a work. Obviously, the sacrament of reconciliation was not in effect yet. She was told by
God to do an action, cease her behavior and obey the law. She likely was very
scared and had a contrite heart, at least one hopes, though the text remains
silent on this score. One hopes after messing up and almost being killed for it
and having an encounter with God, one would repent and walk away from sin.
That is the hope for all of us.

17. Recall Protestants cannot claim apostolic succession because of their
breakaway from the Church in the sixteenth century. Only Catholics and the

that it does in fact matter and have a bearing on our eternal fate. We do not have to be told it also has a bearing on our immediate fate here and now in this life. What a falsehood that has grown up for some because of the unfortunate Protestant Reformation years ago, namely that salvation is by faith alone and everything else is superfluous and what we do ultimately does not matter. One often hears among Protestants that we will go before the judgment seat of Christ, which is biblical and Catholics affirm, but all that matters is that one accepted Christ, so none of what one did on earth will then ultimately matter. What a perverse falsehood. One need only think of the following text in regards to our actions and works mattering as opposed to accepting Christ, being saved, and nothing else matters: Galatians 6:7–8 reads, "Do not be deceived; God is not mocked, for you reap whatever you sow. If you sow to your own flesh, you will reap corruption from the flesh; but if you sow to the Spirit, you will reap eternal life from the Spirit." Could it be any clearer? This text alone refutes the Protestant tenet of justification by faith alone!

It was mentioned already but worthy of a few more lines to emphasize that the Mass does not re-sacrifice Christ, as Protestants often get confused with this notion and some Catholics too to be fair, but it is a sacrifice offered to God recalling the ultimate sacrifice. We then partake in it and in Christ, quite literally through taking in the real presence of Christ in the Eucharist. It is here we join our sacrifice to that of Christ's atoning sacrifice he endured once and for all on the cross. To all that has been discussed in this section, I would add that we humans tend to put God in a box and God is bigger than our finite minds. Christ indeed died for the sins of the world and not an elect group, as the Gospel of John tells us (see John 1:29; cf. 1 John 2:2). Additionally, we are

---

Eastern Churches can claim it. This is not to deny the Church did not need some reform that led up to the breakaway by Luther. The Catholic Church did reform in the Counterreformation, and St. Ignatius of Loyola among others started groups in some way as a reaction to Protestantism. He founded the Jesuits. The Council of Trent was a reaction to the Reformation. It clarified its doctrines in contradistinction to Protestantism and declared many of the Protestant views heretical.

told in terms of eschatology in the Bible that at the end of time all creation is redeemed (cf. Col 1:19–20; Rom 8:19–21). Now, it is pure speculation and not biblical, but perhaps when every knee bows before God (Rom 14:11), there is a time when all people get another chance if we did not take it in this life to repent of our sins and accept Christ, perhaps a last chance to enter into purgatory. However, this is not biblical or a teaching of the church, perhaps just a personal hope for all people, as God is a God of abounding love and grace. And who is to say God is not so gracious that God would withhold such and opportunity from all his children that we are told he loves in the Bible?

We do know no sin can separate us from God and no sin is unforgivable or it would be bigger than God, and we know that is not the case. Recall the giants of the faith and their horrendous sins: Moses killed an Egyptian, David had Uriah the Hittite killed to have his wife, and Paul was involved with the stoning death of Stephen, and yet God not only forgave each of them but also used them to enact his great providential purpose and plan here on earth. Thus, God is a god of grace (*hesed*) and it should be the prayer of all that in the end God will provide us all with more grace than we could ever imagine, particularly in regards to the issue of salvation. The ministry of Jesus and the love and grace he showed humanity certainly suggests this much.

Thus, it has been see the issue of salvation is a bit more complicated than salvation by faith alone, that is, justification by faith alone. Faith is certainly one required component for salvation according to Scripture, but so is baptism, the Eucharist, and doing the will of God, as well as our actions aligning with the commandments of God. Some call the latter works. Scripture tells us we must have all four: faith, baptism, partaking in the Eucharist, and godly actions. Salvation is by God's grace throughout however; this both Catholics and Protestants agree on. So, we must choose God, get baptized (Acts 2:38), eat his flesh and drink his blood to have life in us and do God's will (James). Hence, it is not as simple as salvation by faith alone. That is abundantly clear. One need also recall the importance of forgiveness in our eternal well-being (Matt 6:15;

18:35);[18] this can be understood as one of the works James so adamantly contends is necessary to coincide with faith. Thus, we must work out our faith in fear and trembling (Phil 2:12). The classic Protestant model of salvation by faith alone just does not hold up against Scripture. Some have argued three models of salvation exist in Scripture: Predestination (with its natural corollary of double predestination),[19] Semipelagianism, and Universalism.[20] It is the case all seem to be present, but Scripture must be taken in its

18. Again, it is exceedingly difficult to square these texts in Matthew regarding only being forgiven if we forgive others with the Protestant rallying cry of "justification by faith alone."

19. Double predestination states that if some are predestined for heaven others thus are predestined for hell. Many Calvinists past and present hold to predestination, which is exceedingly hard for many to swallow in light of the implications arising out of double predestination that some people are predestined for damnation or hell to no fault of their own. That is no doubt exceedingly hard to square with a loving God.

20. These three models appearing in the New Testament are cogently explained and demonstrated as existing by the late Reformed theologian Shirely C. Guthrie, *Christian Doctrine*; see ch. 7, "What Does God Want with Us," 118–41. He argues Catholics are Semipelagian, which means God does everything in regards to salvation, but we must do one work, accept Jesus. He is correct in his classification based on using the three models for viewing soteriology. He lays out how each model has its advantages and disadvantages, or perhaps it is better to say positive and negative aspects. A classic augment against the Catholic view by Protestants is that it adheres to a system of "works righteousness." To that, I would say so be it, as that is the testimony of Jesus, Scripture, and the church instituted by Christ. In regards to universalism, meaning the salvation of every soul, one need only recall that the Gospel of John speaks of Jesus being the lamb of God who takes away the sins of the world (John 1:29). After all, the Koine Greek reads sins of the "world" and not an elect circumspect group. John the Baptist utters this upon seeing Jesus for the first time before baptizing him in the Jordan River. If not read in light of the totality of Scripture and not in the context of the rest of the gospel, one can see how easily one might understand this utterance in Holy Scripture as suggesting a universalism where everyone's sins are forgiven and all are saved or destined for heaven. Other texts seem to suggest this view is not consistent with the fuller context of Scripture. There are obviously other texts coming from the mouth of Jesus in the gospels that are hard to square with universalism, regardless of how nice universalism sounds and resonates with most of us, such as those that talk about hell and that speak of weeping and gnashing of teeth (Luke 13:8), scary language indeed.

entirety and texts must not be cherry picked and others ignored. The Catholic view embraces all of Scripture.

Ultimately, one need go to reconciliation and have sins forgiven and remember contrition is requisite to be secure in one's eternal salvation, a salvation that is both of the soul and the body. One often forgets that we have a bodily resurrection as well, which is affirmed at the end of the Apostles' Creed. The ending of it reads, "I believe in the Holy Spirit . . . the resurrection of the body, and the life everlasting. Amen" (cf. 1 Cor 15:35–44; 1 John 3:2).[21] In the end, it is hoped and likely God has more *hesed*, or grace, than we can imagine, for he is God. That is not to argue for a universalism, for other texts in Scripture do not suggest universal salvation is the case, though perhaps that should be the prayer of us all, particularly if we all abide by Christ's summation of the torah when he is asked about which is the greatest commandment of the law. He quotes the Shema (Deut 6:4–5) then a text form Leviticus (Lev 19:18) and distills the torah down to its essence: to love God and neighbor as yourself (Mark 12:28–34; Matt 22:34–46; cf. Luke 10:25–37).[22] To love neighbor as yourself would be to want your neighbor or all of humanity to be reconciled to God through the atoning work of Christ on the cross. God's very being and nature is love (*ahavah* in Hebrew). Mystics past and present have been telling us this for years[23] and so does the Bible, as it explicitly states: "God is love" (1 John 4:8b). Working from a framework of love always would be to follow Jesus' words when he summarizes the torah and this is a yardstick or blueprint by which to judge

21. A helpful article on this topic that contains several quotes from early church writers, entitled "Resurrection of the Body," can be found at: https://www.catholic.com/tract/resurrection-of-the-body.

22. Later rabbinic Judaism articulated a total of 613 laws in the Torah or Pentateuch, that is the first five books of the Bible: Genesis, Exodus, Leviticus, Numbers, and Deuteronomy.

23. Those mystics of the past include St. Francis of Assisi, St. Catherine of Siena, St. Teresa of Avila, St. John of the Cross, Meister Eckhart, Saint Thérèse of Lisieux, St. Faustina and, more recently, Edith Stein, Bede Griffiths, and Thomas Merton. Prominent, popular mystics alive today include the Augustinian Richard Rohr and Father Thomas Keating.

our works, so they align with God and not against his command-ments. And when we do fall short, for we all do (Rom 3:23), we have the assurance of the sacrament of reconciliation and the assurance of forgiveness it provides. It cleanses our souls of the bad works or sins we have committed; thus, going to confession proves, as James argues, "that a person is justified by works and *not by faith alone*" (Jas 2:24).

# Conclusion

IN CONCLUSION, CATHOLICISM EMPHASIZES the mystery of the faith. When speaking about the divine, we can only ever use analogical language that is never remotely adequate. Perhaps that is why, as aforementioned, toward the end of his life St. Thomas Aquinas had some sort of mystical experience and then stated all he had ever written was straw and quit writing. If his writing was "straw" and not adequate in matters pertaining to the Transcendent, as we are finite human beings, then we are at a loss for whose writing can ever do justice to God. But that does not mean we do not try and throw up our hands and not teach the faith to others. The Great Commission that concludes Matthew's Gospel (28:16–20) asks us to go forth and convert, baptizing in the name of the Father, Son, and Holy Spirit.[1] This yet again demonstrates the vital importance of baptism. It has been seen and argued here that the Catholic Church in contradistinction to all Protestant denominations has the fullness of the faith, with its mysteries, and it safeguards its depository of the faith through its tradition. Some may claim it arrogant to possess the fullness of the faith and truth in a secular era,[2]

1. As noted already, scholars agree the Great Commission is original in Matthew and not a later emendation. Though the New Testament does not use the word *trinity*, this text clearly demonstrates a Trinitarian understanding of God that existed since the beginning. The term *trinity* was not coined for the triune God until the Latin theologian Tertullian did so in his writings in the early third century.

2. That our culture is becoming increasingly more secular is without question. I was reminded of this over Christmas, noticing that the television

which understands and propagates a moral relativism.[3] So be it, for it is Christ that we follow and that the Church and all its teachings is found upon, and Christ that ensures its survival and passing on of the faith through apostolic succession!

Ultimately, many of the topics touched on here are profound mysteries of the faith that words can barely do justice to and undoubtedly, not all will agree with what has been advanced here. Recall the Gospel of John says God must first enable us to come to him (6:44). Thus, we do not come to him unless he has enabled us to do so; hence, it is not our own volition that first brings us to God. Therefore, it is not on our own accord that we even believe in the first case; God acts first and then we must respond in faith, via baptism, confessing Jesus is Lord and was resurrected from the dead,[4] and our works must align with God in not sinning

---

networks no longer play movies about Jesus and especially when stopping into a business establishment the other day. While there I noticed a cross with a quote from the well-know text of 1 Cor 13:4–4 on it. I was expecting it to read, "Love is patient, love is kind. It does not envy it does not boast." Instead it read: "Love is patient, love is kind. It does not exist." The individuals in the establishment were very kind people. One may find this trivial, but it is rather symptomatic of an irreverence of all things holy, in this case a beautiful scriptural text usually read at weddings. Countless other examples could be used here, such as movies, sitcoms, or music that openly make fun of anything having to do with religion. It is a sign of the times. Another example of our culture becoming more secular, and in this case hostile to religion, exists in the fishes with legs on them often seen on the back of cars that have the word Darwin written inside it, clearly playing off the Christian fish symbol, as if science and religion are at odds. People using this symbol are often overtly hostile to Christianity but unfortunately laboring under a false assumption that science and religion, in this case Christianity, are at odds. Pope John Paul II was very clear they are not incompatible in the least, particularly in regards to evolution and the book of Genesis, specifically the creation account(s). After all, the church invented science. The problem often, in regards to so many issues, boils down to a lack of education, as in this case.

3. One can also see in the work of Pope Benedict XVI a critique of moral relativism, advancing instead that an objective truth does in fact exist. He was an erudite scholar and his work will be studied for years to come.

4. Recall the important words of Saint Paul noted in this work already regarding the miracle and mystery of the resurrection. First Corinthians 15:14 reads, "And if Christ has not been raised, then our proclamation has been in vain and your faith has been in vain." This is absolutely true; it all hinges on

and attending to the sacraments, especially reconciliation after one has sinned, especially mortally. One should also partake of the Eucharist as often as possible, seeing that it is the very body, blood, soul, and divinity of Christ given to us. It is the blood of the New Covenant Christ commanded us to partake in; the benefits of taking Christ into our being cannot be overstated. Recall what was discussed earlier regarding Jesus' words in John 6:53: "So Jesus said to them, '*Very truly, I tell you, unless you eat the flesh of the Son of Man and drink his blood, you have no life in you.*'"

In a book not widely disseminated in the early church, and some debate existed whether it should even be part of the canon, Jesus likely playing off of Isaiah 43 (cf. 43:18–19) is quoted in the vision as saying, "Behold I am making all things new." The fuller context reads in Revelation 21:5–6:

> And the one who was seated on the throne said, "See, I am making all things new." Also he said, "Write this, for these words are trustworthy and true." Then he said to me, "It is done! I am the Alpha and the Omega, the beginning and the end."

---

whether or not Christ historically was raised from the dead. As Catholics an unequivocal "yes" is the proper answer. If one does not believe Christ rose from the dead, then why be a Christian? One is not a Christian without believing in the resurrection of Christ as Paul explains, for it all hinges on that historical point. Had he not been resurrected, our atonement does not exist. How one answers this question of the historical veracity of the event does indeed have profound implications, as does the question Jesus posed to Peter at Caesarea Philippi of "who do you say that I am," discussed earlier. Seeing Jesus as simply a great spiritual master or sage, as opposed to God who rose from the dead, does not do justice to this figure who traversed first-century Palestine with a message of redemption and love. The world has had plenty of sages and holy men, but only one who provides true redemption. Why believe in another sage, holy man, or rabbi unless he rose from the dead and is God? And this is precisely who Jesus claimed to be—God. This point is virtually on every page of the New Testament in both explicit and implicit ways. Besides biblical evidence, nonbiblical evidence also cogently demonstrates this fact. For such, one should consult Strobel, *Case for Christ*. Thus, one really is not a Christian, a follower of the true "anointed one" of God, unless they believe in the divinity and resurrection of Christ.

He is renewing the earth and all of creation, including each and every one of us. God is always at work, even in the midst of our trials. Everything serves a purpose in God's providential plan (cf. Prov: 19:21; Jer 29:11); we are, thus, not in control.

Other issues not addressed here, such as clerical celibacy and scriptural warrant for it, such as texts suggesting it is better not to marry (cf. Matt 19:10; 1 Cor 7:9), could have been added. Other works can be used to look these issues up, this particular one being a tradition and not an official doctrine. One could argue you want a priest to be completely committed to God and not be distracted and bogged down with mundane matters of the world. With the priestly shortage it remains to be seen if one day Catholic priests will be allowed to marry; in fact, some already are because of special circumstances in which dispensations have been granted for previously married and ordained individuals of other traditions, usually Anglicans, desiring to join the Church. The number is rather small, only a few hundred.

That clerical celibacy is the cause for the abuse of children that has scandalized the church is an untenable argument that exceeds the boundaries of this short work but another important issue to be addressed nonetheless. Suffice it to say that the church is full of sinners in need of God's grace, even the clergy, as no one is without sin (Rom 3:23), and we are to follow the commandments of Jesus and look to him and the teaching of the church, not the few who have sinned grievously and hurt the poorest and most vulnerable.[5] The Church will hopefully, we must pray, address these wrongs. It is without question however that the Church will march on, for Christ is the head of it.[6]

One brief comment is in order: though a priest be a grave sinner, this in no way invalidates any of the sacraments the priest presides over. The Church has been adamant about this teaching, so

5. The pithy expression "do as I say not as I do" or in this case "do as they say not as they do" comes to mind on this score.

6. One of many tangible signs that the church is in fact doing the work of God here on earth can be seen in that the Catholic Church is the largest charitable organization in the world; that indeed says a lot.

we can rest assured the sacraments are always valid no matter the priest and what he has done, for God is always ever present and at work in them. The issues over the Donatist heresy early on in the church addressed this issue and resolved it correctly—the sinfulness of a bishop or priest in no way invalidates the sacrament they preside over. Additionally, God is God and therefore omnipotent and capable of taking care of your every need. God furthermore also knows our hearts when we come to the differing sacraments in which we receive the grace of God. As we are all his children, it is unfathomable he would want to harm rather than heal us and give us his grace when we approach him, however we do that, either through the sacraments or in private prayer (cf. Luke 11:11).

Yet another important subject not addressed here is the incredibly misunderstood topic and history of indulgences in the Church as noted already, for the subject is a bit confusing the first time one is explained it. A limit to this work had to be drawn. Suffice it to say there are plenty of helpful resources out there to address all the objections of Protestants and reveal Catholic truths, including the importance and grace of indulgences.

It has thus been see in this short apologetic work that Reformation tenets are not persuasive or tenable in light of the evidence from the Bible and what has been argued here. For the reasons above, it has been shown that the major issues Protestants have often objected to are addressed by Jesus in favor of the Catholic position and are actually biblical, and the Church since the beginning has affirmed them and passed them on to subsequent generations in an unbroken chain. Christ gave the keys to the Church to safeguard and pass on the faith, which it continues to do to this day. One will have gleaned in this work how regrettable the Protestant Reformation was and how it has led to erroneous and ironically nonbiblical theologies.[7]

Along with passing on the faith to this day, the Church is tasked with the administration of the sacramental system. Just as

7. Ironically, because Protestants have traditionally affirmed *sola Scriptura*, though that is no longer the case with many Protestant denominations today, particularly the mainline ones.

ancient Israel had its sacrificial system, so the Church today has its sacramental system. Israel's sacrificial system offered sacrifices to atone for sin, now the Church today offers the one sacrifice of Christ that its members get to partaken in when they eat and drink the body and blood of their Lord. It is rightly argued as "the source and summit of the Christian life," so Vatican II, the supreme sacrifice offered by the Church today occurs in the Eucharist, and Catholics are at their very core a Eucharistic people. In articulating some of the fundamental doctrines of Catholicism, it has become apparent how Protestant objections to them are not tenable for they are all able to be defended cogently from Scripture, logic, natural law and the teachings of the Church since the very beginning. Writers immediately after the disciples even affirm all the teachings detailed in this work. One can see how because of the biblical evidence, along with evidence from the early church and up to the present, one can argue there is only one tradition that can claim to be the One Holy Catholic and Apostolic Church.

# Bibliography

Akin, Jimmy. "The Woman of Revelation 12." Catholic Answers. May 1, 1997. https://www.catholic.com/magazine/print-edition/the-woman-of-revelation-12.

Anderson, James. *Manifesting Peace: 12 Principles for Cultivating Peace, Healing & Wellness Distilled from the World's Spiritual Traditions and Psychology.* Eugene, OR: Wipf and Stock, 2019.

Bergsma, John. *Stunned by Scripture: How the Bible Made Me Catholic.* Huntington: Our Sunday Visitor, 2018.

Bright, John. *A History of Israel.* 3rd ed. Philadelphia: Westminster, 1981.

Broom, Ed. "Saint Gertrude and the Golden Hail Mary." *Shalom Tidings*, January/February 2019, 15–17.

Catholic Answers. "Resurrection of the Body." Catholic Answers. April 23, 2019. https://www.catholic.com/tract/resurrection-of-the-body.

Catholic Church. *Catechism of the Catholic Church.* 2nd ed. Vatican City: Libreria Editrice Vaticana, 2012.

Cook, William R. *The Catholic Church: A History.* Great Courses Video Series. Chantilly, VA: Teaching Company, 2009.

————. *Francis of Assisi: The Way of Poverty and Humility.* Eugene, OR: Wipf and Stock, 2008.

Dunn, James G. *The New Perspective on Paul.* Grand Rapids: Eerdmans, 2007.

Ehrman, Bart D. *Peter, Paul and Mary Magdalene: The Followers of Jesus in History and Legend.* New York: Oxford University Press, 2006.

Guthrie, Shirely C. *Christian Doctrine.* Rev. ed. Louisville: Westminster John Knox, 1994.

Hahn, Scott, and Kimberly Hahn. *Rome Sweet Home: Our Journey to Catholicism.* San Francisco: Ignatius, 1993.

Horn, Trent. *The Case for Catholicism: Answers to Classic and Contemporary Protestant Objections.* San Francisco: Ignatius, 2017.

————. *Why We're Catholic: Our Reasons for Faith, Hope and Love.* El Cajon, CA: Catholic Answers, 2017.

Howell, Kenneth J. *The Eucharist for Beginners: Sacrament, Sacrifice, and Communion*. San Diego: Catholic Answers, 2006.

Josephus, Flavius. *The Works of Josephus*. Translated by William Whiston. Rev. ed. Peabody: Hendrickson, 1987.

Madrid, Patrick. *Why Be Catholic: Ten Answers to a Very Important Question*. New York: Image, 2014.

McDonald, Lee M., and James S. Sanders, eds. *The Canon Debate*. Peabody: Hendrickson, 2002.

O'Conner, James T. *The Hidden Manna: A Theology of the Eucharist*. 2nd ed. San Francisco: Ignatius, 2005.

Pope Francis. *Amoris Laetitia: On Love in the Family*. Our Sunday Visitor, 2016.

Sanders, E. P. *Paul and Palestinian Judaism: A Comparison of Patterns of Religion*. Minneapolis: Fortress, 1977.

Strobel, Lee. *The Case for Christ: A Journalist's Personal Investigation of the Evidence for Jesus*. Grand Rapid: Zondervan, 1998.

Sungenis, Robert A. *Not by Faith Alone: The Biblical Evidence for of the Catholic Doctrine of Justification*. Queenship Pub, 1997.

Tetlow, Joseph A. *Ignatius Loyola: Spiritual Exercises*. New York: Crossroad, 1992.

United States Conference of Catholic Bishops. *Compendium: Catechism of the Catholic Church*. Vatican City: Libreria Editrice Vaticana, 2006.

VanLandingham, Chris. *Judgement & Justification in Early Judaism and the Apostle Paul*. Peabody: Hendrickson, 2006.

Walker, Williston, et al. *A History of the Christian Church*. 4th ed. New York: Scribner, 1985.

Wegner, Paul D. *The Journey from Texts to Translations: The Origin and Development of the Bible*. Grand Rapids: Baker, 1999.

Woods, Thomas, Jr. *How the Catholic Church Built Western Civilization*. Washington, DC: Regnery, 2012.

9 781532 689031